Foreword by *A.J. HAW*

D0546492

ERRIFIC!
FIVE STAR
CUSTOMER SERVICE ★

Learning About Excellent
Service From Special People

STAN TOLER *&* KEITH HAWK

dustjacket

www.dustjacket.com

ACKNOWLEDGEMENTS

Keith & Stan would like to thank AJ Hawk,
Adam Toler and the entire Dust Jacket team.
What a terrific group to work with!

DEDICATION

In Memory of Kim Hawk

TABLE OF CONTENTS

FOREWORD

I never thought of my Dad's sister, Aunt Kim, as different. She was just my Kimmy after all, but she was unique. Of the more than four million babies born in the United States each year, 340,000 are born with Down syndrome – Kimmy was one of those. And that made her very special.

She was always my biggest fan. From playing for the Elks at Centerville High School to Big Ten football with Ohio State University to starting for the Super Bowl Champion Green Bay Packers, Aunt Kimmy followed my every game. She wore replicas of my jerseys whenever we played, and she knew the game of football almost as well as I did.

Because of her unique perspective, Aunt Kim had much to teach others about how to live their lives. And she could be counted on to give her one-word exhortation to whomever she met: Terrific! To Kim, everyone and everything was Terrific! That's the way she lived every day of her life. To her, life was Terrific!

In the pages of this book, you will meet my dad, Keith Hawk, and his sister Kim, and my friend Stan Toler, as well as two other special people Toni Carter, Stan's niece, and Heather Duvall, daughter of Joe Duvall, friend to both authors. Obviously, they have been inspired by the lives of these special women. From these remarkable people and others, you will gain a great insight on how to treat and serve others.

Further, after reading this book by Keith Hawk and Stan Toler, you will be able to say no matter what is happening around you - life is terrific!

A. J. Hawk
Linebacker, Green Bay Packers
Proud Nephew of Kim Hawk

CHAPTER ONE
Terrific! Five Star Customer Service

I don't know what your destiny will be, but one thing I know: the ones among you who will be really happy are those who have sought and found how to serve. – Albert Schweitzer

I (Stan) travel a great deal and have for the last thirty years. In fact, I've accumulated more than six million miles in airplanes and have earned elite status on several major airlines. On a recent flight, I happened to be seated in coach, not having been upgraded to first class as a member of the airline's executive platinum program. To make up for the change in seating, the airline surprised me by offering dinner.

I immediately said to the flight attendant, "Well, that's great. What are my choices?"

"Yes or No," she quickly replied.

Sad to say, her less-than-enthusiastic response is emblematic of customer service today.

During the more than half century of my life, I have been a keen observer of customer service; over time I've noticed that the attitude of the business world toward that service has changed. Some will say these changes are a natural evolution, the result of a shift from local and national economy to a global economy. Where once we dealt with the owner of a locally owned business around the corner, we may now deal with an international business and its customer service representative on the other side of the world.

No matter the locale and no matter the business, quality customer service should be the norm, not the exception. What are the characteristics of *Terrific!* customer service?

1. Find out what the customer really wants

Some start a business (or organization) certain that they know exactly what their market wants. Unfortunately, they go broke with that certainty still intact. They were willing to gamble their capital on their perception of the marketplace, but obviously perception wasn't enough.

Successful leaders understand that no one knows what people want better than the people themselves. That is why the pillars of our capitalistic system are called "supply and demand."

Customers demand products and services; businesses meet that demand with their supply of products. Businesses research customer needs. But many times customers are trying to describe what they want while they are being brushed off by the goods or service provider thinking the customers must not understand the question because they're not describing the product or service the provider has in mind. Instead of asking, "How can I serve you?" then after the response, saying, "We can make that happen," some ask, "What do you want?" and say (or infer), "No, let me tell you what you want." At the end of the day, the customer will go across the street to someone who will provide what he or she actually wants.

2. Honor the customer

Once I (Stan) was flying to speak at a conference, and as always, I was careful to make sure the conference host had my cell phone number and knew that I would wait for them at the baggage claim. When I landed in the airport, I turned my cell phone on, and there was a voicemail from the conference director: "As you know, this is a large conference, Dr. Toler, and we have over 6,000 people in attendance. I'm sorry to tell you that I won't be able to pick you up personally. But I want you to go to the baggage claim and *look for someone who looks like they're looking for you.*"

Well, I don't know if you've ever gone to a baggage claim, but *everyone* there looks like they're looking for someone! When I found my way to the waiting area, no one seemed to be looking for me. I waited . . . and waited . . . until finally everyone had left. I came to the conclusion that no one was looking for me.

Finally, a man came toward the baggage area holding up a rumpled, yellow piece of scrap paper. On it there were large, scribbled words written with a permanent marker . . . "STAND TALLER." Now the sign gave me smile, because people often mispronounce "Stan Toler" and end up calling me "Stand Taller." When they do, I usually joke, "I'm trying! I'm trying!"

As amused as I was by his sign, I was a little disappointed when we got the bags to the curb. There, instead of being transported to my hotel in a reasonably well-kept auto, my chauffeur added my luggage to a collection of stuff in the bed of his unwashed, dented pickup truck. It was a leveling experience.

Of course, I was grateful I had a ride to the hotel—and expressed that to my driver—but I confess that during the trip, I was playing armchair quarterback about the director's welcoming call.

Everyone wants to be treated as if what they do is important.

If customers have a choice between a business or organization that respects their needs with quality, respectful service and one that gives them careless service and doesn't meet their needs, they'll go with the first option every time.

Contrast that experience with another one later on:

I was about to go on a trip and needed to get my oil changed before I left. My regular mechanic was out of town, so I wanted to find a local shop that specialized in routine (and quick) automotive maintenance. About a half mile from my house are two such businesses. I walked into the first one and asked the clerk behind the counter, "Will you change the oil in my car for $22.99?"

I knew this was the price of their oil change because a big sign behind her listed all their services and prices. But her response told me so much more than the sign. "We can, if that is what you really want." I knew immediately that she was trying to leverage services. She was absolutely certain she knew what I wanted more than I did. The sign behind her was not a contract with her customers, but rather a catalyst to convince me of buying more than I had intended.

She began her sales pitch to convince me of what I needed. As she was talking, I turned around and began to walk out. She called out to me, "I thought you wanted your oil changed!" My response was simply, "No, thank you."

I got back in the car and drove about two hundred yards down the same street to a similar franchise. I pulled up to the garage door, and this time I didn't even have to get out of my car. A young man enthusiastically bounded out to greet me, "Can I help you?" As I approached the oil change business, I had seen a young man out on the corner holding a sign with the price. But as I usually do, I still asked the obvious question: "Do you do oil changes for $19.99?" This time the response was totally different from their competitors'.

"We do that all day!" he responded.

He asked for my keys, and I got out and walked inside to the small waiting area. They never questioned the type of service or the price. I will say that over the next few minutes, they tried to up-sell me twice—and succeeded once. When they told me I needed a new air filter I bought one (the evidence they presented was conclusive).

What made the difference in where I got my car serviced? The employee at the first business questioned if I really knew what I wanted while the employees at the second showed respect for my judgment. Although they gave me additional options, their attitude was, "We are here to give you everything you need to service your car." I ended up spending as much or more money with them than I likely would have spent down the street. But their attitude toward me as a customer was totally different, and that's what won them my business.

There is an old saying about the two rules of customer service, "*Rule number one: The customer is always right. Rule number two:* If you ever doubt the customer, refer back to rule number one."

Nowadays it seems the motto is, "Rule number one: *we're* always right. Rule number two, if you doubt that statement, refer back to rule number one." It's not a matter of education; it's a matter of expectation. The customer expects to have his or her needs met in a way that suits them. It doesn't mean customers are not open to options; it just means they are looking for confirmation and connection, not confrontation.

3. Confirm the customer

Jill Griffin, who writes and speaks about marketing and customer loyalty, says, "First time buyers are testers and they look for confirmation that they feel they have made a good decision."

Good customer service allows the customer to try things out. If you've been to an ice cream shop recently, you remember a couple of things. First, all of the ice cream isn't the same flavor—there are varieties of ice cream and toppings. I guess you could say "one ice cream doesn't fit all!"

The second thing you may notice is that you can try that ice cream on for *size* (unless you're going for the fat free, sugar free, taste free option.) On top of the counter is a container with very small plastic or wooden spoons inside, and a stack of tiny cups nearby. Choose a flavor and the attendant will give you a spoon or cup full of the ice cream free of charge.

The ice cream may typically sell for three to five dollars per cup or cone. Over a month's time, the owners of the shop may give away a lot of very expensive ice cream as samples. But they understand the value of connecting with their customers through their product. By letting their customers try the product, they are confirming their customer's decision to spend money on ice cream is a good one.

My brother, Mark, walked into an ice cream parlor, and other than the employee at the counter, he was the only person in the place. He stood at the counter while the employee seemed to ignore him and kept on polishing a milk shake machine.

Finally, Mark gave the employee a rather loud, "AHEM!" When the employee turned around, he said to her jokingly, "Are you going to serve me, or not?"

The employee's response was a classic. She pointed to a plastic number dispenser on the counter and said, "I'm sorry; you'll have to take a number." (Some would say that's enough to melt your ice cream!)

Customers are samplers. They often will come into our business or organization to try them out for size. During Stan's many years as a pastor, he taught his regular attenders to always respond in the same way to questions from guests about where something was located: "I'm going that way, let me take you."

When I (Stan) was a young pastor in Florida, I didn't have very many adults in the church—it was mostly teens and children—and most of my adults were very actively involved in ministry assignments. One week I determined that I needed to spend more time before the service in preparation for delivering the message and organizing the service; so I would stand at the door and shake hands after the service rather than before. That meant I needed to recruit a greeter. I thought, "Who is the friendliest person in my church?"

Immediately I thought of eight-year-old Walter Rutherford, who was the cutest kid in the world and as friendly as a pup. So one day I said to him, "Walter, I want you to be my head usher."

He always called me "Preacher," so he said, "Preacher, what's an usher?"

I told him what an usher did, and he said he thought he could do it. The Sunday morning he became my head usher, he was standing at the door of that small church in Tampa wearing a beautiful red blazer—his grandmother had dressed him up like a million bucks. I had told him, "Now, if anyone new comes in, I want you to let me know and introduce them to me."

Well, he did me one better than that. I was up front getting organized, talking to the worship leader, when all of a sudden I heard him yell out, with his hands cupped around his mouth, "PREACHER, PREACHER! LOOK HERE! WE GOT SOME BRAND NEW CUSTOMERS!"

And six brand-new "customers" walked through the door!

I had to work with him on that line and teach him to say "guests" rather than "customers." But he definitely got the spirit of what I was looking for.

I have shared this story with church leaders many times over the years. I tell them, "You need to be like Walter. You need to make sure you meet the guests, know who they are and where they're from, and always be helpful in every manner. Servant leadership cannot be overestimated. Helpfulness is paramount, and, even in church, the five stars of customer service should always be practiced.

Do a little bit more

I have found some of the best illustrations of customer service in what would seem at first to be unlikely sources. Actually, people with special needs often have character qualities that connect with others in astounding ways. Their innate friendliness and concern connect with people way apart from their own challenges.

The first example comes from a member of my family, a niece named Toni. Like Kim Hawk, Toni Carter was born with Down syndrome. As we write this, she is forty-seven years old and has lived much longer than the doctors expected. Though she has certainly experienced the physical challenges common to people with her condition, she is fully able to care for herself.

The National Association for Down Syndrome describes some of the challenges Down syndrome children face:

> *Many children with Down syndrome have health complications beyond the usual childhood illnesses. Approximately 40% of the children have congenital heart defects. It is very important that an echocardiogram be performed on all newborns with Down syndrome in order to identify any serious cardiac problems that might be present. Some of the heart conditions require surgery while others only require careful monitoring. Children with Down syndrome*

have a higher incidence of infection, respiratory, vision and hearing problems as well as thyroid and other medical conditions. However, with appropriate medical care most children and adults with Down syndrome can lead healthy lives. The average life expectancy of individuals with Down syndrome is 55 years, with many living into their sixties and seventies.

Toni is the living embodiment of what Elizabeth T. King said, "I find that it is not the circumstances in which we are placed, but the spirit in which we face them, that constitutes our comfort." With her persistence and positive attitude, she offers a strong example of the surprising gifts that anyone can bring to our society.

Toni's customers

Working at a Taco Bell restaurant in her hometown every weekday afternoon, Toni has developed a group of loyal customers who come to her restaurant partly to receive the service she provides. She knows them well and greets them as they come in for a soft drink or taco. They are much more than customers to her; they are like family or close friends.

Toni's unconquerable spirit and willingness to meet every challenge are an inspiration to everyone. People are uplifted just being in her presence.

But she also displays outstanding business practices. She may not have an MBA, but she understands some business principles better than many who have directed corporations for years. One of the most important things she teaches is how to provide good customer service.

Not long ago, Toni was selected as the Waycross Chamber of Commerce Employee of the Year. Among the more than fifty thousand people who call that part of Georgia home, she was the one the chamber felt should be honored above everyone else. They presented her with a plaque during a banquet and used flowery words to describe the qualities of a young woman who, without a college education or specialized training, was affecting so many lives in a positive way.

Later, after the banquet was over and she had received her plaque, I asked if she had any words to share about how she won the award. What was it that made her stand out from all of the others? She told me three things:

- Number 1: Refill drinks.
- Number 2: Smile really big for the customers.
- Number 3: Get lots of tips.

Wow! The wisdom she possesses defies the wisdom of many great thinkers the world over!

Let's look more closely at her explanation.

She refills drinks.

How many people understand the importance of good, attentive customer service at such a simple level? Toni understands that even in a fast-food restaurant where few expect any kind of customer service.

> People value the small things, and consideration and attention to detail will encourage them to come back again and again.

Many times even at a full-service restaurant with china, silver, and cloth napkins, getting the waiter or waitress' attention to get a tea glass refilled is like trying to feed a carrot to a racehorse in the middle of the Kentucky Derby— yet the servers expect a good tip at the end of the evening. But when a simple Styrofoam cup is refilled at Toni's restaurant, it's done with as much care and attention as an upscale restaurant in Beverly Hills.

She also makes an effort to remember which brand of soda they drink and the amount of ice they use and also makes sure they have a straw. When someone makes such an obvious effort, the value of the service heightens. Customers feel honored to receive that kind of treatment.

Toni feels good as well, because she knows the people she serves appreciate what she does. It is a win/win business experience.

> One of the greatest things someone can do for another is to give them value.

Toni smiles "really big"

In addition to refilling her customers' drinks, Toni offers them a smile that seems to come from the very depths of her soul. Think about it, smiles are getting rare in the world today. Yes, there are smiles scattered about on most business days, but they are very often impersonal and perfunctory— like the smiles people sometimes give to someone in the grocery line, or the forced smile of cash register attendant at a busy restaurant. To demonstrate proper etiquette, they may say "Thank you" or "Have a nice day" and look pleasant for the required few seconds and then look away. These are the smiles of duty rather than delight.

Toni gives her customers a million dollar smile with a one dollar drink that they will remember for the rest of the day.

> She has learned that if she wants an uncommon response from her customers, she has to give them an uncommon or unexpected reaction to their business.

She practices the words of Amway founder Richard DeVos: "Few things in the world are more powerful than a positive push—a smile. A word of optimism and hope, a 'you can do it!' when things are tough." She goes the extra mile in every area of the service she provides, and that includes the smile customers receive when they first walk in the door.

How much would your service to customers improve if they felt you genuinely demonstrated an appreciation for their patronage? You've probably heard the story of the restaurant patron who said to the waiter, "Do you serve crabs here?" With an enthusiastic smile, the waiter quickly responded, "Oh, yes sir. We serve anyone!"

We have become a society that takes things for granted. People believe they deserve their job, their home, their car, their cable television, and almost anything else that makes their life more pleasurable and convenient. In the past, people felt that nearly everything in life had to be earned in some way (and maybe that wasn't all bad).

- If there was a roof over their head, they had to build it themselves or find the resources to purchase it from someone else who had the skills to build it.

- If there was food on the table, they grew it themselves or earned wages at a job that allowed them to purchase it from someone who had the means to grow it.

- If they couldn't afford a car, they rode the bus or walked.

- Television was a luxury that they could live without if they couldn't afford it.

When we earned some of those things, we were genuinely pleased with our progress in life. Now, most of them are expected. This has taken away the joy and satisfaction of earning our successes.

Toni experiences joy each time she smiles at a customer, and they smile back with the same enthusiasm. She has the satisfaction of knowing she has earned her customer's smiles.

Toni gets lots of tips

Toni has discovered the personal fulfillment of a proper reward for an appropriate effort. Author A. Lou Vickery describes it this way: "Four short words sum up what has lifted most successful individuals above the crowd: a little bit more. They did all that was expected of them and a little bit more." Toni's effort is an example of those four words, *a little bit more*. In a world of doing no more than necessary, or no more than absolutely required, Toni wants to give more than is expected. As a result, she reaps a harvest from the seeds of extra effort she has planted.

4. Set the pace

There are usually two groups of people in the workplace. The first sit by and wait for a *green light*. Theirs is a world of waiting and watching, analyzing and agonizing. Some of them wouldn't know an open door if it had a flashing neon sign on it.

The second group takes the initiative. They're on the move—waiting for a *red light*. They have an idea (or borrowed one from someone else) and put a joyous energy in gear—and they keep on going till they come to a red light. Of course, they're still concerned with the bottom line; otherwise they wouldn't be good team members. But they spend more time doing what needs to be done rather than thinking about what should have been done.

Toni is in the second group—she takes the joyous initiative. She is not sitting by and asking or waiting for someone else to provide for her. She has the self-respect afforded someone who is self-reliant. She has earned the right to look in the mirror and feel good, both about who she is and what she's done.

For example, Toni doesn't see her tips as the charity of others but rather a reward for a job well done. Some people take charity and assume it is their right. Not Toni, she knows without a doubt that she has done the right thing—no matter how small her efforts may be. It's the little acts of customer care that result in customer loyalty.

5. Do it right or don't do it at all

Terrific customer service doesn't just happen—it's anticipated. Written into the business plan of successful ventures are achievable goals, stepping stones to the final objectives. And one of the most important goals has to do with quality service.

> If your organization's only concern is quantity, you will end up with neither quality nor quantity—and the customer will be the victim of a drive-by idea.

CHAPTER TWO
Connection: A Winning Attitude

Intensity and effort are the two things I can control.
- A. J. Hawk

Kim Hawk valued others over herself in tangible ways. When she turned 16, and her parents, Dean and Mary Hawk, gave her a birthday party at a local restaurant, more than 100 people came to honor her. Even though the invitation said not to bring presents, many brought gifts anyway.

Kimmy's reaction to the presents was interesting. She was sad that she was the only one who got to take something home from the party. From that time forward, whenever there would be a party for her, she insisted on going to a "dollar store" to buy something for each person who was invited. She didn't want them to leave empty-handed. She made an instant connection.

Genuine concern for others is the cornerstone of great customer service.

Kim Hawk was a personification of that concern. Our friend and best-selling author, John C. Maxwell, often said in his leadership seminars, "People don't care how much you know until they know how much you care." And that care is a cornerstone of customer service.

Clean restroom test

A noted traveler and speaker told the story of a first visit to a five-star restaurant. He said as soon as he was seated at a table, he excused himself and visited the restroom. He has the unique policy of visiting the restroom at a new restaurant before he places his order. His thinking is that if the restroom isn't clean, it isn't likely the kitchen is clean either! Once the restaurant passes the cleanliness test, he goes back to his table and orders his meal.

He said the new restaurant exceeded all his expectations.

- The facility had a pleasant fragrance.

- A courteous attendant stood inside, charged with the task of making certain the place was clean and meeting the customer's needs and expectations greeted him.

- The attendant turned the water on at the sink to just the right temperature, provided liquid soap for hand washing, and offered a clean, white towel for drying. Then he offered a spray of cologne and a sterilized comb.

The customer gave the attendant a generous tip and was invited to come back soon. He added, "When I walked out I knew that it was very likely that I would return."

The restroom attendant had made a customer connection that wouldn't be forgotten. In fact, the speaker not only made a return visit to the well-known restaurant, but the business has received numerous mentions in his seminars and in his writing, as one that truly cares about customer service.

Again, *Terrific!* Five Star customer service gives attention to the finest details.

Kim Hawk had a talent for connecting with others. How was she able to do this?

- First, she genuinely cared about them.
- Second, she always worked hard to please them.

When she suffered a stroke, she was sent to physical therapy. Kim loved going to PT. She worked hard to do all that was asked of her, and those working with her connected with her because of it. But once her insurance benefits ran out, she couldn't continue to go. Her parents knew how disappointed she would be. To Kim, not going would seem to be letting down the physical therapists who asked so much of her.

Her father Dean Hawk spoke to one of the workers at the facility and told them that Kimmy would not be coming back. He had a special request of them: Could they please make up a certificate that announced she had "graduated" from physical therapy? Not only did the good people who had worked with Kimmy do this, they also threw her a party. She left feeling very good that she had made her therapists and other personnel happy. Kim may well be the only person to have officially graduated from physical therapy!

She had made a conscious connection.

Her great sense of connection exemplifies some important principles.

Practice conscious connection

Practice is repetitive, purposeful actions that result in positive reactions. A football team that doesn't have a purpose-driven practice schedule eventually won't have a schedule at all—they won't be around when the championship trophy is handed out. Champions know that a constant rehearsing of the fundamentals is a key to the personal success of each player—and the team itself. They consciously focus on doing the right things at the right moment.

Super Bowl-winning coach Tony Dungy said in a talk to his players, "You have to understand that all the little things your coaches are asking of you really do matter. Knowing I count on you is just as important to me as your talent. You'll always find excuses for not doing exactly what you are supposed to do. But that's exactly what creates a losing environment."

It's the same in leadership of all kinds. How do you practice conscious connection? There are at least three important things that must be done to connect with your customers.

1. Listen to them

Listening is more than giving a polite nod to the words that come from someone's mouth. It involves the total person.

Listening is a lost art in our culture. We have communication devices everywhere, but few people are truly listening.

The late, great communicator Erma Bombeck said it best: "It seemed rather incongruous that in a society of super-sophisticated communication, we often suffer from a shortage of listeners."

Erma passed away before the preponderance of iPods, cell phones and Bluetooth ear pieces. I am sure she would have said something amusing about the state of listening in our digital age. But sometimes it's not that amusing. It is not uncommon to go to dinner and find two people texting or talking on their phones during the entire meal. Some even text to the person sitting or standing across from them!

We choose our communication channel—the music we want to hear, the words we want to hear—and adjust the volume according to our tastes.

Grow through listening

With our own agenda already set, our pocket-sized devices serve as personal genies, granting us audio wishes at our command.

The problem is that it totally inhibits personal growth. Listening to others with our full attention, we are able to share in their experiences—and grow by them.

Listening is integral to connecting. It helps us understand the life experiences of another.

Listening is so much more than hearing: it is receiving and understanding the message the other person is sharing with us.

Once someone has truly listened, they can reflect on what was said. This reflection may take moments or minutes. It may require deep thought or just a passing contemplation. Sometimes people are sharing something that requires us to make an immediate response, such as a congratulatory remark or a word of sympathy. When people are pouring out their heart about something important to them, too often the people listening are waiting for a break in the conversation so they can try to top them with a story about their experiences. It's better to listen "clear through," and then carefully respond. The result is "value-added listening" for both the speaker and the listener.

Whether you are a leader or a follower, listening is a must.

No one learns anything by talking or writing. All learning is done by listening or reading.

It is amazing what people will share with a relative stranger in a restaurant, their hairdresser, or someone sitting next to them in an airport or hospital waiting room. Those unguarded moments often create an opportunity for a listener who is objective to provide an opinion that person could never get from friends or family.

Listen with your mind by focusing intently on what the customer is saying. You may want to include some focus principles, such as repeating their words in your mind. If you knew you would be required to repeat what they said out loud, you would pay close attention to their train of thought.

Listen with your ears by paying attention to the tone of the customer's voice. Your customers come from a variety of life experiences—some painful, while others are pleasant. By paying attention to the tone of their voice you can respond in a way that will heal their hurts or share their triumph.

Listen with your eyes by making eye contact with the customer. In this digital and impersonal world, eye contact is often ignored. A case in point is when a vendor makes change with one customer while talking on the phone to another. The person who made an effort to come to the place of business is essentially put on hold while the customer who didn't make the same effort is given preferential service.

Listening with your eyes also allows you to look for the hidden needs or wants of the customer. Couples in a relationship, for instance, can speak to each other with their eyes. One look can convey such things as approval, disapproval, uncertainty, or expectation.

Listen with your body by moving toward the customer. Your very stance is an indicator of your interest in your customer. *Standing away* rather than *moving toward* could very well make the difference in a sale or a "No, thank you." Think back to the people you know that are great listeners. If they are in the office, they might be the ones who put their hands or elbows on the desk and lean toward you as you talk. Conversely, they probably won't be the ones who listen with their arms folded defensively.

Good listeners are mobile. They move toward and with the customer or the inquirer, rather than allowing that person to take a self-guided tour around their goods or services.

2. Show genuine concern about them

Those with Down syndrome are usually known for their warm and caring attitude toward others. Theirs is a world of smiles and hugs and compassion. In fact, they have an "UP syndrome" heart for others.

Toni Carter may not be a trained counselor, but she has common sense in her approach to her Taco Bell customers. She reflects carefully on what they say and responds to them honestly and openly.

Toni is a friend to her customers:

- She cares for them unconditionally.

- She makes an effort to remember their names.

- She remembers their life events.

- She shares their concerns.

Acting upon the needs and concerns of others takes less time than you might think. Businesses and organizations are learning about the value of sending a thank you note or following up with a brief phone call.

Toni gives value to her customers by listening to them earnestly. She recognizes that they need her to be a friend at that time. Other times she may just give them an embrace or a kind word of encouragement. She will let them know in some way that she cares. It doesn't take much time. And it doesn't hurt business—it helps it.

3. Celebrate victories

Kim Hawk attracted people to her by being genuinely interested in them. She enjoyed all that went on around her, especially parties and celebrations. "We were the only family to celebrate Groundhog's Day *Eve*," says Kim's father.

Terrific! customer service looks for celebrations to share. For example, if a customer gives you the scoop on such things as a job promotion, community recognition, or a family milestone, share the joy—be a part of the victory celebration.

Those celebrations may even call for an "added value" item or service, but you can be sure that your investment and sharing in the victory will not be forgotten.

4. Walk the extra mile.

These days it seems like customers almost expect poor service. You've heard the comments about fast food restaurant personnel. In some fast food establishments your retirement benefits could kick-in before the wait staff gets your order right.

> Connecting with customers not only requires efficiency, it requires empathy. A little bit of listening and caring could go a long way in offsetting botched services.

We all have interacted with numerous sales and service workers over the years. All of these people see hundreds, if not thousands, of other customers. They do not have to take the time to remember who we are or anything about our needs. If they didn't, we would still have the need to buy clothes, have things dry cleaned, or eat out, and we might still use their establishments. But they understand that going the extra mile will pay dividends in our purchases and recommendations. Customer service counts.

The U. S. government projects an increase of service jobs through 2018, "The shift in the U.S. economy away from goods-producing in favor of service-providing is expected to continue. Service-providing industries are anticipated to generate approximately 14.5 million new wage and salary jobs."

So many chances to serve! And so many opportunities to connect! But the key link will be putting the "serve" in service. *Terrific!* customer service will remain dependent on those who have a heart to serve, not just a knowledge of service.

The noted educator and historian Charles Francis Adams said it well: "No one ever attains very eminent success by simply doing what is required of him; it is the amount and excellence of what is over and above the required that determines the greatness of ultimate distinction."

CHAPTER THREE
Creativity: A Valuable Experience

There is but one use of power and it is to serve people.
- George W. Bush

Jon Aton was pictured, in the February 27, 2012 issue of Time magazine, sitting at his desk in the Massachusetts statehouse. He serves there as an intern to a state representative and gives guidance on issues relating to developmental disabilities. Previously he visited Washington D. C. and had his picture taken in front of the White House. Inscribed beneath the photo in his scrapbook were his words, "This is my future home."

Jon works creatively as an advocate for those who have developmental issues. It's an area of expertise for him. He was born with Down syndrome. In 2010, he was named Down Syndrome Congress Advocate of the year.

His advisor says his work ethic has everyone talking about him, and adds, "It's not something you can buy. It's something inside."

Creativity is a first-level requirement for the success of any business or organization.

You've seen the familiar Greyhound busses on the road. One of their early slogans said, "When you focus on basic needs, you're always needed." The slogan was often used to inspire vision in leadership training but in 1990 the company filed for reorganization under Chapter 11.

Soon after, two passengers on an airline flight made their introductions and began to ask about the other's vocation. One of the passengers introduced himself as an executive with Greyhound. The other passenger, an author and officer in a national leadership training organization replied, "That's interesting, I use your slogan as an illustration when I teach leadership seminars."

"What slogan is that?" the executive asked, and then proceeded to suggest several of his corporate slogans— to no avail. Finally, he admitted he didn't know to which slogan his seatmate was referring.

The leadership teacher answered, "When you focus on basic needs, you're always needed." The Greyhound exec looked surprised. "I've worked for this company for many years, and I have never heard that slogan," he continued, "We're in bankruptcy now, and we desperately need to apply that principle to the company. When I get back to the office I'm going to call a meeting and remind my staff about that slogan."

Perhaps history proves the influence of that chance meeting and the discussion of the business strategy. Greyhound soon emerged from bankruptcy; who knows whether the reminder of the company's original focus was a factor in their getting back on the road to recovery.

Whatever the organization, whether General Motors, Garmin, or Google, when it focuses on customer needs and creatively tries to meet those needs, it will always have a market.

The singular quality of American businesses is creativity. We have developed innovations that have startled the world. A noted business professor once said that the moment an organization ceases to become creative it starts to slide backward.

This has been demonstrated in business time and time again.

In recent times, the lack of creativity has brought down some of the mightiest corporations in history.

- **General Motors** once was the largest and strongest company in the world. Its financial strength equaled—or exceeded—that of a mid- sized nation. But, in 2009, GM filed for bankruptcy and came under government control.

- **Sears** was once the envy of the retail world. Its corporate headquarters in Chicago encompassed over three billion square feet in one of the tallest buildings in the nation—a symbol of its corporate power. In the last few years, however, Sears has declined and has closed stores across the nation—and the Sears Tower has been sold.

- There was a time when most everyone wanted to own an **IBM** personal computer. Even competitors' products were known as "IBM clones." But IBM has now sold its personal computer division to Chinese investors. In a market where personal computers are said to be re-invented every eighteen months, IBM struggled to keep up.

These are just three examples of companies once counted among the most innovative in their fields. Their triumphs have been overshadowed by their competitors: Toyota, Wal-Mart, and Apple respectively—companies that have changed the marketplace. They were creative while the former companies were complacent.

The case for creativity

Complacency is the enemy of creativity. Jim Collins describes this dynamic in his book, *Good to Great: Why Some Companies Make the Leap and Others Don't*. He writes of the quality of leadership and the principles that take companies from incompetence to greatness, the discipline and technology factors that will raise companies above their competitors, and the change and restructuring companies endure to get to the next level.

Further, Collins suggests that creativity is not a matter of technology, but a matter of leadership and company culture. People develop creative ideas not because they are smarter than the rest of us, but because they care more about their end users. They look for new ways to resolve the needs of their customers. This is the secret of anyone who desires to impact customers:

Always look for ways to improve a customer's experience

Is there room for creativity even in the small confines of a fast food restaurant? You might not think so but the opposite is true. We heard of a man who went to a neighborhood fast food restaurant and was surprised when the counter person asked his first name. He had been to the establishment many times and had never been asked that question. He complied and gave them his name—curious about the new custom. He soon discovered the answer. When the order was rung up, his name was displayed on the cash register's new monitor that faced the customer. On the display was "Welcome to . . ." and the customer's name. Personalized and creative customer care!

The birth of creativity

Creativity can be born in any venture if we will just put forth the effort. For example, Taco Bell is continually trying to find new menu items that stay within their overall brand but offer new options for their customers. In fact, customers are often given the opportunity to be a part of the menu expansion. It only strengthens their bond with the company.

In a Harvard Business School article, authors James Allen, Frederick F. Reichheld, and Barney Hamilton propose that great companies design right offers and experiences for the right customers and develop capabilities to please customers again and again.

So, the key factor in a successful business is that it is customer-driven, not company-driven. The company takes every creative step necessary to meet the needs of the customer.

It will use focus groups and surveys to enhance its knowledge of its end users. It will recognize that the core question is not, "How can I improve the profitability of the company?" The question is, "How can I best serve my customer?"

A recent visit by Keith to Google, which is one of the world's fastest growing and most successful organizations, revealed a corporate motto, "focus on the user and all else will follow." They went on to explain that since the company started they have focused on the best user experience possible.

> The more creative a company is in solving and resolving the issues of their customer, the better the customer and the company will be served.

The wholesaler, Sam's Club, is a real world example of this principle.

A nonprofit organization in the Midwest sent one of its administrative assistants to a nearby Sam's Club for office and kitchen supplies. Because the organization was tax exempt, the employee was required to show a copy of its federal tax exemption paperwork. The Sam's Club card used to purchase the supplies also identified the holder as representing the nonprofit.

Each time she made a purchase, the cashier appeared to be suspicious of her, as if she was lying to avoid paying a few dollars of sales taxes. Over a period of time, the employee began to dread going to the store to purchase the supplies.

Since she shopped for supplies at around the same time of day, it seemed she would always have the same sales associate for the check-out—and receive the same stressful treatment.

One day she went to Sam's Club, purchased the needed supplies, and again was given the third degree by the sales associate. But, on that day, everything would change. As she was walking out of the store, the store manager walked up to her and asked if everything had gone well with her shopping experience. She took the moment to tell the manager about her ongoing experience with this particular associate. She described how she dreaded coming to the store and encountering the same questions and distrust. She said that if it weren't for the prices, she wouldn't have returned.

The manager assured her this was not the way that Sam's Club treats their customers—and was advised that she would never have that experience again. A day or so later the sales associate with whom she had experienced all of the difficulties came to the organization's office with a box of chocolates, a dozen red roses, and a written apology. She had been suspended for a day without pay and had been told by her manager that she had to make it right with the customer or her job was in jeopardy.

The story of what happened spread throughout the organization. Not only were the employers surprised that the business would take such immediate action, they expressed a new loyalty to Sam's Club. This is a great example of a company taking the steps to make their customers happy.

The concern of creativity

If the twenty-first century has taught businesses anything, it is that the organizations who have defied the pendulum swings of the economy have done so through creatively serving the needs of the consumers.

Author Steve Denning reflected on the leadership of the late Steve Jobs in a *Forbes* magazine article, "The most profound contribution that Steve Jobs made was in demonstrating a radically new way of running a company: the goal of the firm shifts from making money for the shareholders to delighting the customer. As Jobs said: 'My passion has been to build an enduring company where people were motivated to make great products.' The products, not the profits, were the motivation."

> The genius of Steve Jobs was that he was always bringing products to market that fulfilled needs people didn't even know they had.

One thing that sets Apple apart is its creative approach to customer service. When an Apple customer has a question about a product,

- They will call a toll-free number provided by the company.

- They will speak to a live person.

- During the course of the conversation, the Apple representative will give the customer a direct phone number and e-mail address for future reference.

- If any further issues arise, the customer can directly contact the representative they have dealt with before to resolve the issue.

- With Apple, there is no waiting in line or talking to someone who speaks only passable English (though many other companies consider this the height of customer service).

Apple does not take any shortcuts in providing quality customer service. Take your iPad to their service center and, in moments, they might replace it with one with a wireless system that works correctly—no questions asked!

The five steps required to provide excellent customer service are:

1. Preparation.
2. Concentration.
3. Incubation.
4. Illumination.
5. Verification.

Preparation: Passion and Examination

Saying that creativity requires preparation might seem almost contradictory—isn't creativity spontaneous? But, in truth, being prepared is an integral part of being creative. The easiest thing in the world is to keep doing what has always worked in the past. We feel more secure when we do something we know and understand.

When people get together to think of new ideas, rehashing old ideas is often the first step taken. This is why creativity requires real preparation. We have to do the work of opening our minds and our hearts to the possibilities around us. We must open our minds; if we cannot conceive something in our mind, we won't be able to create it. Andrew Carnegie said, "Whatever your mind can conceive and believe it can achieve!"

But the beginning point is the conception—discovering the idea. We must also open our hearts because the creative process is an emotional progression as well. We tend to fall in love with our best ideas; we become emotionally attached to them and don't want to turn them loose! The most creative people are also the most passionate.

A significant part of preparation is learning all of the available options. This is important because we begin to learn the strengths and weaknesses of the options already present.

> ## Some of the best ideas in the world come from combining ideas that didn't work separately, but together are explosive.

Only by surveying all the options can we see ways to combine them and take them to a new level. Also, by looking at the available choices, we begin to understand why they might not work as well as they should. Before we can begin to understand what will work best, we have to understand what does not work.

You might want to use the SWOT analysis: a strategic planning method used to evaluate the Strengths, Weaknesses/limitations, Opportunities, and Threats involved in a venture and then define your objectives:

- **S**trengths: characteristics of the business, or project team that give it an advantage over others

- **W**eaknesses (or Limitations): are characteristics that place the team at a disadvantage relative to others

- **O**pportunities: *external* chances to improve performance (i.e. make greater profits) in the environment

- Threats: *external* elements in the environment that could cause trouble for the business or project

Creative preparation requires us to look at things in a different way. We are looking afresh at things we see every day with the purpose of pulling out useful concepts. In some products and services, we will want to take things apart—both literally and figuratively—so that we can see what makes them work.

Today, products are being continually examined to see which parts are not essential. And there is a continual drive to make the products smaller, while continuing to improve their quality.

If you are trying to improve service, you may want to take a field trip. Go somewhere that offers great service and see what they do well, or go somewhere where the service is considered bad and see how they earned that reputation. You may want to list the steps to good service or the opposite steps to bad service. It may seem strange to list the steps of bad service, but that allows us to dissect the process of serving customers and learn from it. In the process, we'll find the essential steps to quality. We find the steps in our processes that can never be skipped. We see where a service might get off track or leave out essential elements. We learn what not to do. This can be every bit as important as learning what to do.

Preparation: Adaptation and Observation

I (Stan) met my friend Terry Bates on a Tuesday morning for breakfast. When the waiter came to our table, I ordered the oatmeal with sliced bananas and raisins and wheat toast with butter on the side. My friend said, "Ditto that with a cup of coffee, and I'll be a happy person."

In a little bit, our food came out, and we noticed that we had white toast, not whole wheat toast, and almost in unison we said, "We ordered whole wheat toast."

And the server said in his own interesting way, "We *ain't* had *no* whole wheat toast since Sunday morning." In other words, their supplier wasn't informed of the need.

Now mind you, this is a breakfast restaurant WITHOUT ANY WHOLE WHEAT TOAST! Again almost in unison we said, "Well, that store across the street would have whole wheat bread."

The person didn't get it nor did management, apparently. After the meal, I told Terry that I nearly left and bought a loaf of bread to take back to the restaurant, just to show them what customer service is all about. And he said, "You know, I had the same thought. It would have been funny if we both showed up at that place with a loaf of whole wheat bread."

What this breakfast place didn't get:

Serving customers means looking for solutions outside your standard operating procedures.

If customers want wheat toast instead of white, find a way to get them wheat, even if it takes you away from your usual ordering and stocking routine.

Another way to prepare for creativity is to get away from the norm. The old saying that we are often "too close to the forest to see the trees" really applies here. Albert Einstein said, "You cannot solve problems with the same level of thinking that creates them."

Preparing for creativity allows us to escape from our ordinary routine and do the uncommon. There is a reason that successful people will often be found checking out their competition. They are not spying; they are learning what works or doesn't work somewhere else. For example, when entrepreneurs go on vacation:

- Decorators will look at homes and shops.
- Car dealers will look at car lots and dealerships.
- Pastors will visit other churches.
- Writers will hang out in bookstores.

They are always looking for ideas. That is one of the foundations of their success.

Some have called this process "pause and notice." There must be a time when we purposefully stop to observe the things around us.

Looking and Observing

Many do not succeed because they are looking instead of observing, Looking is simply acknowledging that something is there. Observing, on the other hand, is not merely acknowledging, but also genuinely understanding all of the facets of what is seen. It is the understanding that makes the difference.

Often we go through life not really seeing things until something happens to bring them to our attention. Perhaps we look at a certain style of clothing, then all of the sudden we are seeing that style everywhere. We may drive a certain make or model or color of car and then begin to see that type of car all around us on the highways. We have begun to pause and notice.

Helen Keller said, "It is a terrible thing to see and have no vision."

So many people go through life seeing, but not envisioning the possibilities all around them.

Preparation: Implementation

The final step in preparing for creativity is giving ideas a chance to be born. Deep within our souls are all sorts of ideas that are just waiting to escape. We must find a way to allow those creative innovations to see the light of day. Creative people are constantly wondering how they can do things differently. For example;

- Actors like performing in live theater because they can continually try new acting techniques. They strive to reach the edge of their creativity.

- Chefs love to cook, and for them, going to a restaurant includes evaluating the ingredients of the entrees ordered. They may think as they eat: with a cup of this or a pinch of that, this food would taste so much better.

All of us have thought about ways we could improve many of the things we do. But as usual, remembering what we want to remember is more challenging with every birthday. We would be better off to write the ideas down and get them out of our heads. Evaluated later, they may not seem as perfect as we first thought—but expressing them may be the seed for a better idea. Many of us have been preparing to be creative for a long time.

When we do that we may well discover that some of those very ideas are amazingly practical. We can be staggered by our own creativity. Think of the simplest inventions that have impacted our culture:

> ## We need to let pent-up ideas out of our head and heart and into the real world.

- Toothpick
- Clothespin
- Coat hanger
- Pocket comb
- Stapler
- Safety pin
- Scissors
- Pencil
- Paper clip
- Band aid

Concentration: Undistracted Focus

After we have taken the step of preparation, we begin the phase of concentration. Creativity can be hard work—and some people may not be willing to clock in. Moving to the next level isn't for the weak or the lazy. Birthing good ideas takes a concentrated effort. It takes meticulous focus on every detail. Nothing can be overlooked.

There is a difference between people who achieve good things and people who achieve great things. That difference is often the degree of concentration they give their ideas and passions.

One of the things that set Kim Hawk apart from most people is the amount of concentration she devoted to the task at hand. There was no question that whatever she was doing at any given moment received her full and undivided attention.

We are a world of multitaskers. We drive down the road talking on our cell phones (in those states or provinces that still allow it) while listening to our iPods and taking sips from Styrofoam coffee cups filled with coffee we paid for with a coupon found on our tablet computer. We've even added a new item on the citations handed to us by the friendly officers of the law: driving while distracted.

If we're not careful, we'll become a "jack of all trades but master of none." Mastery of anything requires our undivided attention. It is not something we do by accident or when our schedules permit, it is something we do on purpose—consistently.

One of the most amazing things about creativity is that the harder we work at it, the more likely we are to discover other things accidentally.

For example, those Post-it notes we use to remind us to pick up a gallon of milk on the way home from the office were developed by someone trying to create stronger glue.

Later, the same lab created super glue. Similar accidental inventions throughout history are myriad and legendary-all sorts of products, from Coca-Cola to potato chips to ice cream cones, were made accidentally. Other everyday products, like galvanized rubber and plastics, were accidents as well. The individuals involved were focused on doing a great job, which allowed them to realize the great possibilities around them. Concentrating on the task opens all of the creative possibilities.

It does seem oxymoronic to say that if we concentrate enough accidents will happen, but truth is often stranger than fiction.

Incubation: The Perfect Blend

The third phase of creativity is incubation. This is where the ingredients of the idea are being stirred around to see what will work, and what will not. The incubation phase is essential to creativity.

We prepare for creativity and open our minds and hearts as much as possible. We focus on the task at hand, open to every possibility. Then we let our creative idea develop until we arrive at just the right innovation that will be a possible world changer. Some of the best recipes, business ideas, and working relationships have come from people using a little bit of this and a little bit of that.

A cook, for example, will keep adding and mixing ingredients until the taste is perfect. It's the same in the creativity process. We bring together a number of pieces from several ideas, and after a time come up with the right solution.

At other times, our creative innovation is a single idea. We might be eating pizza at our favorite Italian restaurant by day or trying to fully digest its mix of onions and pepperoni during the night. Suddenly the light shines in— the proverbial idea bulb begins to glow.

Some would call the moment a "Damascus Road" experience, like the New Testament hero Saul (later known as Paul) experienced on his way to the capitol for documentation with which to carry on his tirade against Christian believers. Suddenly a blinding light knocked him off his high horse and sent him sprawling.

It was a life changing encounter. Arguably, Paul was one of the most innovative leaders in church history, but his sudden enlightenment was followed by a period of incubation. After his Damascus Road experience, Paul spent three years learning, and letting his new ideals flesh out in his life.

The result could be dangerous at best. Incubation is easy to skip, but doing so will come with a great price. Remember Coca-Cola's "New Coke?" It was a *Wow!* that turned into a *Whoa!*

> Without giving our Wows!—our ideas—time to develop into our "What nows?"—time to brew and prepare for our "What ifs?"—we might try to implement an unfinished idea to bring change.

Probably the researchers did their research and the developers did their developing. The marketers marketed and the advertisers advertised. But someone forgot to tell the customers what a great idea it would be to change the branding of the ages old soft drink.

Launched in April of 1985, it was pulled off the market by June of the same year. Sam Craig, professor of marketing and international business at the Stern School of Business at New York University, pointed to what he and other industry observers have long considered a fatal mistake on Coca-Cola's part. "They didn't ask the critical question of Coke users: Do you want a new Coke? By failing to ask that critical question, they had to backpedal very quickly."

Illumination: Building Enthusiasm

After incubation is illumination. This is a process whereby an idea or innovation takes form in your mind and in the minds of others. This is the moment when you see movement that becomes a real possibility. You may share your idea with a friend or a group of friends, and everyone jumps on it. It has been described as an "Aha!" or "Eureka!" moment.

It is the moment when the thinker becomes impressed with his or her own idea or innovation. It may seem self-serving to be impressed with yourself, but . . .

If you do not begin to believe in what you are doing, no one else will ever believe in you either.

The illumination phase creates excitement and enthusiasm necessary to put ideas In motion to make them viable in the real world. Every day, great ideas come across the minds of thousands, ideas that have the potential to change lives. But only a small fraction of those are ever implemented in a practical, effective way.

How many times have you heard about a new program or invention and said to yourself, *I thought of that but didn't do anything about it*? Perhaps you thought it wouldn't work or you had a lot of other things going on at the time and never got around to fleshing the idea out and trying to implement it.

There are ideas all around us. We have to shine a light on them.

Sometimes when a new idea is announced, the first reaction is, "Why do we need this product or service?" Be aware that when the first personal computers were introduced, the universal reaction was, "Why?" The public responded similarly when telephones, televisions, and radio were first made available. But someone thought these products would eventually be used universally. They had an *illumination* moment when everything was clear to them about what their idea was and what it could do.

Any great idea starts with one person who understands it *fully* and begins to tell the world *clearly*. Illumination is a type of conversion experience where we become totally committed to something that has the power to change lives in some way. That is why sometimes the early adopters of an idea can be called "evangelists." They will tell the world about their idea because their minds have become illuminated, and they want to see the great things that will happen if the idea is adopted and accepted.

Verification: Real-life Application

The final phase of creativity is verification. There has to be a time and place where an idea is verified as life changing by people other than its creators. At this time, the idea begins to take form and others have the opportunity to verify that it works.

- If it is an idea for a physical product, a prototype is built and used to determine if it works and what flaws it might have.

- If it is a service, the idea is tried on a small group, sometimes called a focus group, to determine how well users accept it.

- In the academic world, there is something called "peer review." A professor or researcher writes a paper describing their research, methods, and findings regarding a particular subject.

- Their academic peers will examine the research and determine if the outcome seems valid.

- In business, there is product testing. Developers will give a group of people samples of the product and ask its members if they like or dislike it, and why.

- In political campaigns, voting groups listen to a speech or watch a debate and give their reactions to campaign staff.

As you can see, for just about every type of product or service, there is a way to verify new ideas. The verification process is an important phase. If the creative idea cannot survive the verification process, it is not yet perfected. Soliciting input from others allows for a fresh perspective. Others may have input which is invaluable in taking the idea from good to great.

Sometimes this critiquing and tweaking process happens over a very long period of time. Computers, for example, are constantly evolving. Once they filled an entire room. Later, desktop computers were as common as desk chairs. Then, the first laptop computers became a must-have. Now, the smartphone—a pocket size computer—you might have in your jacket or purse can outperform the computer that once filled a room.

It is hard to think of a product—from bath soap to automobiles—that has not been improved by the input of others. Ideas that make sense to some people will not appeal to others at all.

The perfection of an idea requires effective application.

Some great concepts do not work as well as anticipated when put into practice. They make perfect sense in theory, but when the time comes for them to be used by others, all sorts of problems arise.

Likewise, other ideas seem unworkable at the outset, but when they're placed into application or production, everyone wonders why no one thought of it before. This is why the application or verification phase of the creative process cannot be overlooked.

If we're going to accomplish anything great in life, we cannot neglect the whole creative process. People are always looking for shortcuts to make things work, ways to avoid steps in the process. But the reality is that, though skipping steps may work on occasion, eventually those who use shortcuts will get burned.

There is a short poem that describes the complete process:

> Successful people possess a balance of creativity and character.
> They have enough creativity to think it out.
> They have enough character to try it out.
> They have enough creativity to feel it out.
> They have enough character to find it.
> They have enough creativity to picture it.
> They have enough character to produce it.

Enough said.

CHAPTER FOUR
Centricity: A Personal Touch

You cannot continuously improve interdependent systems and processes until you progressively perfect interdependent, interpersonal relationships.
- Stephen Covey

Friends of both authors, Joe and Peggy Duvall have a lovely daughter named Heather who was born with Down syndrome. Heather graduated from Washington Court House Local Schools in 2004 and then attended Laurel Oaks Vocational School for two years, completing her studies in early childhood education. Soon she began work with the Fayette County Head Start program as a Center assistant.

Her job involves helping children choose their daily work and assisting them in learning the alphabet, name recognition, colors, shapes, cleaning and setting tables for meals, as well as anything else she is asked to do. In fact, as soon as she sees her boss, she will ask, "What do you need me to do?"

Heather is a marvelous example of someone who understands centricity. She loves people and loves her job; she always centers on people and her work. Recently, she wrote down her "Eight Principles to Live By" and gave us permission to share them in this book.

1. Keep smiling all day long.

2. Keep saying to yourself, "Have a good day."

3. Love your job and do it right.

4. Work is a game so make it fun.

5. Make sure your light shines throughout the day.

6. Remember you are there to help the children learn.

7. Keep your energy up all day long.

8. Do these every day of the week.

Heather gets it when it comes to having a great outlook on life and a great understanding of the importance of centering on people.

The opposite example may be found in a business traveler's experience at a sandwich shop in an airport terminal. He recalled, "I went to the counter quite hungry.

I hadn't eaten all day, and I had a flight to catch and needed to grab a bite quickly. I ordered a plain turkey sandwich on their special bread, and was careful to say, "No dressing, no mayo, no veggies; just meat and bread, please."

He said the cashier gave him a drink cup to get his Diet Coke and chips, which he did, and joined several others who were waiting for their food. His story continued "as a big, burly cook fixed the sandwiches and called out order numbers, I sat and ate my low-fat chips and drank my Diet Coke. When he hollered, 'Number 66,' I walked over, thanked him for my sandwich, and sat down. But, when I unwrapped the sandwich, I observed that mayonnaise was oozing out of it I walked over to him and said, 'Sir, my sandwich has mayonnaise on it . . . I said no mayonnaise.'

The cook said, 'Well, then you should have ordered it plain.'

I started to reply, but he interrupted and said, 'If you want something like that you have to tell the cashier that's the way you want it. I have no way of knowing that.'

He went on for quite some time. I could not get a word in edgewise.

Finally he got to the end of his lecture, and I said, 'Look, I know what I told the cashier, and you're most welcome to discuss that with her. What I really want right now is a plain turkey sandwich, just bread and turkey and that's all—two pieces of bread and meat.' And I smiled.

He said, 'I will fix you a plain turkey sandwich.' Then he picked up the sandwich and hurled it about twenty feet across the room, where it hit a trash can with a resounding thud and fell on the floor. And he turned and went into the back to prepare me my plain turkey sandwich. At that moment I realized I did not want him to prepare me a plain turkey sandwich. So I went on my way."

Returning to the airport for another trip, the same customer passed by the same restaurant, at about the same time as the last—and was just as hungry. But he decided to skip the turkey sandwich and the lecture. (He was *fed up* from the last visit!)

Now the core issue wasn't mayonnaise. It was the cook's attitude. He cared more about pushing his agenda than serving his customer.

Heather Duvall is all about "centricity"—making sure her students are at the center of her attention. When she is at work, she cares most about job issues that relate to those in her charge. She wants to make sure they know she cares about them, and that she has given them a big smile. That is what makes her such a valued member of the workforce.

Marketplace Attitudes

Three different attitudes are far too common in customer service today.

1. "We don't care about you." (And it shows.)

The cook at the airport sandwich shop is a prime example. He didn't have to hold up a sign. It was written all over his actions: "We don't care about you!" But it shows up in other settings as well. For example, corporations may exhibit that attitude in the way they treat customers, associates, and their employees.

They believe building a financial base is more important than building a customer base. But historically, this prioritizing has not held up. It has been proven that businesses that purposefully care for their customers will have a better chance of surviving economic downturns.

2. "You are a number and we are here to process you."

Businesses often measure their customer service, not by the customer's with their product or service, but by how little time the company spends with the customer. In the business world this is called "average handling time." Employees will be assigned an average time they should spend satisfying the needs of their customers. If they spend more than the allotted time, they might even face disciplinary action. As a result, the employees are focused on getting the customers offline or off the phone from the moment the conversation begins. Whatever issues the customer may have are secondary in businesses that have not yet discovered the importance of constantly adding to the value their customers receive.

3. "We care, but we're clueless."

The third attitude is illustrated by a dry cleaner that I (Stan) use all the time. My wife says that I only use them because they call me "Sugar" and "Darling" and "Sweetie." They are very nice to me and read my books, so that very well may be true.

Not too long ago, I dropped off some shirts. When I went to pick them up, the clerk at the front desk said, "We have a little problem with one of your items—your monogrammed shirt. Someone burned a hole in the middle of the back. You probably wouldn't want to wear it like that, would you?"

The answer wasn't that much of a stretch. "No, I don't think so."

So the lady behind the counter said, "Well, honey, we'll get you a new shirt or we'll get you a check—if the shirt is custom made."

I told her it was custom made, and she said, "Well, then, we'll get you a check."

I will never forget the letter that I received from the cleaners' corporate office about six weeks later. It was the mother of all form letters. It looked like it had been typed on a manual typewriter with half of its keys sticking. I've never seen such a messy letter in all my life. It even contained form letter prompts like "insert title" and "insert first name"—they hadn't responded to any of them. They'd just typed my name in and stamped the customer service director's signature at the bottom, without properly filling in any contact information.

A fifty-dollar check fell out of the letter, which led me to remain a customer of the business establishment. But the experience reminded me that . . .

> ## Some organizations say they care, but don't have a clue as to how they do it.

My impression of the dry cleaner shop owner is this: somewhere in the training process, someone forgot to teach that person about quality care. As someone with a large hole in the back of a monogrammed, custom made shirt, I would be a little more impressed if someone had made a bit more dignified effort to express remorse for botching the job.

Opportunity and Approach

Some corporations view customer service as a problem to be dealt with, and not as an opportunity to serve others. If anything, they view it as an opportunity to push products or services that the customer may not even want or need—added profit rather than added value.

"Having the lowest price in the market is not a sustainable advantage. It can be trumped at any time by a determined competitor. Though all customers want the feeling that they are getting a good deal, they do not buy because of the deal. They buy because they are seeking to fix a problem in their business, to start a new revenue opportunity, or to make a business process easier."

Customer service is given lip service while the sales presentation becomes the primary focus of the customer-business interaction. If service agents increase their orders, awards and recognition will follow.

Heather Duvall takes a totally different approach with her students, "Remember, you are there to help." Toni Carter has a similar attitude toward her Taco Bell customers. She is there to help them with a refill and a smile. She doesn't try to sell them up. The customer is the center of her attention. For this the people of her community have recognized her. Toni's attention to the needs of her customers brings them back for more. Her efforts to serve drive more business than any "upsell" campaign could ever accomplish.

Great companies make service the center of their approach to customers. The department store, Nordstrom, is known for its customer service. A poster in a Nordstrom store in San Diego describes their attitude in a few words: "The only difference between stores is the way they treat their customers."

A mutual friend of the authors had this motto demonstrated to him firsthand at the San Diego Nordstrom store. He was looking for a gift and stopped in to find it. Looking all over the store without success, he started to leave. An outgoing young lady with a Nordstrom name tag asked him if he needed help. He briefly described what he wanted to purchase. She assured him Nordstrom did not have the item he described.

The nice young lady told him not to worry. Although Nordstrom did not have the gift, there was a Talbots store nearby. She told him that not only did they have what he wanted, but she knew exactly where it was in the store and would go there and pick up the gift for him. The sales associate armed him with a magazine and a diet drink, took his credit card, and away she went.

A few minutes after she left he began to have second thoughts about sending a complete stranger away with his credit card, but it was too late by then to do anything about it. But by the time the diet drink was gone, the young lady had returned with the exact item he had been looking for, wrapped and ready to go. That day she convinced our friend that he should always go to Nordstrom when he wants good service from a department store. They truly do treat their customers differently than many other stores. Nordstrom understands the principle of listening to customers.

Upside-Down Thinking

This quality of service is rare these days. We live in an upside-down world. Good service exists in some services that are not always essential and doesn't exist in other services that are absolutely essential to the way we live. Some have reminded us in humorous ways, such as: Only in America can you get a pizza to your house faster than an ambulance.

And only in America do drugstores make sick people walk all the way to the back of the store to get their prescriptions.

A bank will open both doors to their vault all day, but chain the pens to the counters. It's like they're saying, "Take all the money you want, but LEAVE OUR PENS!" Talk about misplaced priorities. A book could be written about displaced priorities in America, but then it might seem as if displacing priorities is a priority.

Others say grocery stores are places that make almost no sense at all. They sell hot dogs ten to the package, while they offer hot dog buns in packages of eight. The store forces us either to buy two packages of buns or to throw away two hot dogs! It would seem that some bakery would want to package ten buns together and corner the market or that a meat company would increase the number of frankfurters to match the packaging of the buns. It's not even the different packaging that's so bothersome, but the fact that no one seems to care!

And that's the real bad news about all of this: we take it without a complaint. We have become so accustomed to bad service or bad products or bad packaging that we don't even think about it anymore. Likewise, we have become so accustomed to poor customer service that it is no longer a priority for us to find good service.

> People can be disappointed only so many times before they stop expecting good things—so they can avoid further disappointment.

We have hardened ourselves to avoid a feeling of frustration.

Changing the Status Quo

But the good news is that some companies are determined to change our expectations. They are determined to stake a claim in the marketplace by being different from their competition in their approach to customer service. When there is a challenge in the marketplace, they rise to meet it. Corporate trainer Kate Zabriskie said, "Although your customers won't love you if you give bad service, your competitors will!"

Companies are determined to take advantage of the vacuum in customer service. In the middle of the first decade of the twenty-first century, several things happened which would eventually separate the survivors from the insolvent.

A crisis developed in the consumer electronic industry because of two events. Electronic retail outlets had been making record profits selling new flat-screen televisions to consumers. The televisions were pricey but envied and desired by nearly everyone. Anyone who could afford a new television was maxing out their credit card and buying one. It was the biggest consumer revolution in electronics since the introduction of color television nearly a half century earlier.

The demand grew. More manufacturers, not wanting to miss the opportunity, began to start production of these items. New companies came online. More and more televisions were manufactured. And prices began to drop like a stone in the water. Nearly every month, the prices of televisions fell a little more. Sometimes the stores would have inventory in stock that was only a few weeks old, but they had spent more wholesale than the retail prices being offered by their competition. Because of a smaller profit per unit, the contest became about moving inventory quickly while controlling overhead.

Along with the growing demand by consumers, the second contributing factor was the availability of consumer electronics by big-box discount retailers like Wal-Mart and Target. Even wholesale clubs like Sam's and Costco entered the business. All the competition pushed the prices even lower. The pressure on retailers like Best Buy and Circuit City became intense. They were looking for every way possible to beat the competition. Each took a different approach, one that would determine their ultimate future.

Best Buy decided they were going to do everything they could to provide the ultimate electronic buying experience for consumers. Their plan was to target five types of highly valuable customers:

1. Affluent professionals who wanted the best technology and entertainment experience.

2. Active younger males who wanted the latest technology and entertainment.

3. Family men who wanted technology to improve their lives—practical adopters of technology and entertainment.

4. Busy suburban moms who wanted to enrich their children's lives with technology and entertainment.

5. Small-business customers who wanted to use Best Buy's products and services to enhance the profitability of their businesses.

They remodeled their stores after their new strategy with this goal: enhancing the shopping experience in their stores. Originally, they tried it in 32 stores. After achieving success in those stores, they expanded it to an additional 110 stores. They called their approach a "customer-centricity" effort.

- They offered a setup for those who wanted to experience a home-theater system with a complete audio and video package.

- They provided gamers the opportunity to try new games in all available consoles.

- They presented other electronics in consumer-friendly ways, including personal computers and appliances.

- Each department had well-trained associates standing nearby to happily answer any questions about their products.

- Besides just being armed with product knowledge, the employees were empowered to make on-site changes they felt would better serve the particular customers who walked into their store.

- Employees in one store reconfigured the home appliance department to create a home-like atmosphere.

- They also created a child's play area in that department where kids could play while their parents shopped for a new refrigerator. Sales in that department grew by double digits.

- To help the more serious customers with their electronic issues, Best Buy created a specialty group called the "Geek Squad." These specialists were to assist with everything from computers to video theaters.

To sum it up, Best Buy decided they could not go toe-to-toe with the discount stores on price, but they could offer a quality of service the consumer would be willing to pay for. This has opened the door to some very upscale customers who are looking for the highest home entertainment experience they could find. Plus, those items have a substantial profit margin.

The Wrong Approach

When the market originally became tight on electronics, the closest national competitor to Best Buy was Circuit City. And they took a different approach to the competition game.

The decision was made to cut costs to the bone and compete on price alone. They decided that, in order to compete, they had to lower their overhead cost. Wages being the highest single item of overhead, slashing payroll lowered overhead dramatically.

- They fired many of the employees they had nurtured over the years and replaced them with new employees hired at lower wages.

- They also decided to increase traffic to the stores by offering the lowest prices on new-release DVDs on the market.

- At the same time, they would keep other overhead costs low by bunching products together in the smallest square footage possible.

Unfortunately, there were negative results to their plan. Customers might walk into a Circuit City store to purchase a DVD and see an electronic product that caught their eye. But, because of the downsizing of the support staff, they often encountered a salesperson who knew very little about it. Rarely could buyers find someone to help explain the finer features of a product.

As Wal-Mart, Target, and other discount retailers entered the market, Circuit City found it increasingly difficult to keep up. The discount stores met the price challenge on the DVDs and other products; with the volume discounts the discount stores were able to obtain, Circuit City struggled to compete on price. They had committed to a strategy of drawing customers and staying above the fray on price alone, but this was a struggle, and the discounters offered just as much customer service as they did. Soon, Circuit City was floundering, and in the fall of 2008, they declared bankruptcy and closed their doors.

Best Buy, meanwhile, was weathering the storm nicely. They offered a competitive price on products as well as knowledgeable customer service. This had been their goal all along: to offer the service their customers needed. Thus, they improved bottom line profits in the midst of the worst global economy in modern day history.

The Power of Indispensability

Former Stanford professor and business writer extra-ordinaire Tom Peters has made a career of profiling companies of all sizes across the country that have made a difference in their profits by rising above their competition in the area of customer service. He says the only way success can be measured is by how well they serve their customers. Peters understands that good service is more than simply serving the customer; it is creating an experience the customer will never forget. He says that the gold standard in selling is to be indispensable to the client - no other goal is worthy.

The word indispensable sums everything up. This is the characteristic that sets certain companies apart in regard to their customer service. Companies who depend upon price and selection soon discover there is always a competitor who has a bigger selection and is willing to slash prices and cut their profit margins to the bone. The companies who become indispensable to their customers *because of their service* create unshakable customer loyalty. When approached by other companies, their customers respond, "You may be able to provide the product at a better price, but you cannot do for me what they do for me."

When the interaction with customers is so outstanding that it is shared with friends and family, a firm has reached the ultimate in customer service. People love to get together and talk about all of the bad experiences they've had with customer service. But when a positive experience rises to the level of being worthy of telling others, it becomes a wow.

The WOW Factor

Speaking a few years ago in Oklahoma City, Peters talked about the "WOW factor." He called it "the Pursuit of WOW!" He defined the "WOW!" factor as "stepping out from the crowd of look-alikes and doing things differently."

Tom believes it should be the goal of everyone to hit a home run in customer service every time they step up to the plate. It is well understood that no one hits a home run every time, but if you never strive to hit one, you are unlikely to ever do so. A firm should endeavor to deliver the "WOW" experience every time it interacts with its customers. NFL Hall of Fame and former Heisman Trophy winner Roger Staubach once said at a Fellowship of Christian Athletes Association event: "There are no traffic jams along the extra mile."

> In every business, it is possible to find a way to provide a "WOW" experience for the customers.

Even if you're a behind-the-scenes player in the business of sports and entertainment, it is possible to determine what would provide a "WOW" experience for fans. Many people think the only way is to provide a winning team on the field. But there are ways besides winning to create a memorable experience.

When the new Yankee Stadium opened in 2009, it featured a large concourse between gates 4 and 6. That alone provides a "WOW" experience for everyone who walks through it. Then there are the seven-story ceilings above the 31,000 square feet of retail space and the banners of past and present Yankee superstars. There is the humongous LED ribbon, five feet high by three-hundred-and-eighty-three feet long. In addition, there is Monument Park, where all of the retired numbers of Yankee superstars for nearly a century stand in all their glory. Win or lose, fans get a "WOW" experience when attending a game at Yankee stadium.

Making the customer the center of everything is the foundation for excellent customer service. Providing excellent customer service isn't always the chosen concept of modern marketing executives.

CHAPTER FIVE
Community: A Team Atmosphere

Individual commitment to a group effort—that is what makes a team work, a company work, a society work, a civilization work. - Vince Lombardi

Not all superstars play professional sports. Some impact their local communities by encouraging others to excel in spite of their challenges. Their weaknesses join with the strength of others in forming a world-changing team. Erika Kissel was born with Down syndrome, but her excitement about life and living is a contagious *UP syndrome* attitude. She not only graduated high school, she has taken classes in theater arts and performs with a community theater group. But her main interest is sports, "I'm a sports fanatic," she says.

> *When I was younger, I was on the park district's softball team. In 7th and 8th grade, I was part of the cheerleading squad. I really enjoyed going to all the games to cheer. I now cheer with the Tomahawks Cheerleaders for the hockey team. When my brother-in-law, Jay coached volleyball at Bartlett High School I was a team manager for the girls' volleyball team. I am involved with Special Olympics sports through WDSRA (Western DuPage Special Rec. Association) I enjoy all of my sports activities!"*

Throughout history there has been one constant among successful businesses: the *combined efforts* of a good team. In the early agrarian society, the team was the family. Everyone worked in the fields, doing various chores from dawn to dusk. Everyone had a job and played a role in the success of the endeavor.

As society evolved, skilled tradesmen would bring in an apprentice who would become a part of the team. As the apprentice learned the trade, he rose to master the skill and eventually led everyone in the shop. These same societies also developed military forces where soldiers were divided into groups with leaders who directed the team. The teamwork in the military continues much the same way to this day. Nearly every area of our society works better with a team of people rather than an individual. As Doug Smith said, "Teams share the burden and divide the grief."

It doesn't matter whether the battlefront is the stadium, the farm fields or the boardroom; teamwork is what makes things work at their peak. Today we often glamorize the individual who appears to be setting the record, making the sale, or starring in the movie. But, in reality, no one ever achieves success alone. We are quickly determining that the sum is bigger than any individual.

The Green Bay Packers overcame the adversity of 15 injured players on the disabled list to preserve and win Super Bowl XLV in February 2012. As one team official said, "every time a star player would go down with an injury, he was replaced by a role player who said, "how can I help us win?" For sure, the role players solidified the unified commitment to truly perform as a team and became their ultimate success.

A motivated group of individuals committed to being a team will always outperform a group of people who are each determined to be the star.

Basketball great Michael Jordan once said, "There are plenty of teams in every sport that have great players and never win titles. Most of the time, those players aren't willing to sacrifice for the greater good of the team. The funny thing is, in the end, their unwillingness to sacrifice only makes individual goals more difficult to achieve. One thing I believe to the fullest is that if you think and achieve as a team, the individual accolades will take care of themselves. Talent wins games, but teamwork and intelligence wins championships."

Consider these "team" scenarios:

- Sports teams – Professional athletic clubs combine the skills of many into a team of one, and have fans that follow their teamwork religiously.

- Political teams - Candidates put together "teams" of individuals with unique talents but who share their ideas and ideals, and who work together to make sure their candidate is elected.

- Corporate teams - A new CEO will often bring in his or her own team of specialists in finance, marketing, production, research, and other areas of business to work together for a common mission.

Winning Teamwork

For the last century, sports teams have been one of society's best examples of teamwork. In nearly every sport a team will often come from the lowest ranking to win a major title. When fans and sports writers evaluate their achievement, they usually conclude it was because they played as a team. There might not have been one "star" player on the team, but his or her "stardom" was in their team play. The sum of the parts was greater than any individual effort.

Teams excel because they share the joys and disappointments together. They win and lose as a team.

But behind the team members is a coach or team of coaches who affirm team talents and cheer them on in wins or losses. Teams who feel appreciated strive to make a stronger and better contribution to the team.

William James once said, "The deepest principle in human nature is the craving to be appreciated."

So, as team members are appreciated—and appreciate each other—they begin to work harder and contribute more. It becomes a kind of perpetual motion machine where, the more the team works together, the more they contribute; and the more their contribution is affirmed the greater the team's possibility for success.

Companies understand the role this dynamic plays in organizational efficiency. One example is the airline, JetBlue.

JetBlue and the Principles of Leadership

In an industry known for its ongoing labor disputes and falling revenues, JetBlue became known for its teamwork and strong bottom line. The airline was initially founded to fill a niche in the market by featuring perks such as leather seats and satellite TV.

In the difficult time after 9/11, the company saw unusual growth. But by 2002, the company realized their goal of strong customer service was not being met. Due to a growth spurt and high customer demands, they had hired new employees and thrust them into service before they were ready.

The JetBlue leadership team decided they were not going to allow their objective of strong customer service to go unmet. To solve their problem, they created a leadership development plan that would train every employee and share organizational values such as customer service.

JetBlue based the leadership program on five principles:

1. Treat people right.
2. Do the right thing.
3. Communicate with your team.
4. Encourage initiative and innovation.
5. Inspire greatness in others.

Armed with these principles, leadership opened the door to rapid growth while maintaining quality customer service. Implementing these Principles of Leadership, or POL as they are called, has led JetBlue to become an organization where both customers and team members feel valued and appreciated.

Because of the success of POL, JetBlue airline employees began to be transformed into a community. Just as in any community, the members served in varied roles but each was important to the success of the whole. At JetBlue, they understand that the pilot cannot fly the jet without a mechanic maintaining the airworthiness and safety of the planes. Likewise, someone must sell the tickets, or there will be no passengers and no one will have a job.

JetBlue determined that a key to their success was in everyone working as a team, with the same values, goals and mission. Without question, their leadership training program has been the centerpiece of their success.

The eBay Explosion

Another notable business community, one that has sprung out of the interest in e-commerce in the last decade, is eBay. This web-based organization has created one of the largest and most diverse business communities on planet earth, with expected revenue of $13 billion by 2013. People all over the world now go online and offer items for sale. The sale is coordinated between seller and buyer. The price of the goods being sold is collected and passed on to the seller with a fee for eBay. The items are then shipped from the seller to the buyer. All of this is done without face-to-face meetings.

The connection between the customer and the retailer is a virtual one.

To operate, eBay needs a variety of team members, from Web designers to quality control specialists to marketing managers to language interpreters. The company now has specialists in e-commerce whose job descriptions were not even imagined just a few years ago.

In truth, without teamwork, eBay wouldn't work at all. Imagine the confusion if there were no team members working to coordinate inventory, design marketing, develop delivery systems, or answer online questions so people could find what they were looking for?

Their team-driven innovations allow customers to sell products easily. Imagine if the only way buyers and sellers could make a transaction was solely through mailing or receiving a hard copy check? Sellers would wait for the check to clear before they would ship the product, slowing down the whole process. A simple sale of a book or camera might take weeks or months. As a result, people would probably not use the service because of the length of time involved for the product to arrive.

In every step of the eBay experience, from the time a product is advertised online until its delivery to the end user, each person's role is vital.

B. C. Clark family-business teamwork

Another example of teamwork is found in a local, family-owned business. The role of family teamwork on a farm was previously mentioned. But this is only one example of how families work together from generation to generation.

There are notable examples of family-business teamwork in the corporate world, like the Ford family in the auto industry or the Johnson family in household products. In Oklahoma, there is a group of jewelry stores that have been family owned and operated for well over a century. B. C. Clark opened a jewelry store in downtown Oklahoma City only three years after the city was established. That was fifteen years before statehood. Obviously, many other businesses started in the city during those first years of its existence, but B. C. Clark Jewelers is the only one still surviving.

Store manager Lane Roberds said the store was created on two principles: family and excellence. To this day, those principles are still demonstrated. B. C. Clark, Jr., worked in the store for nearly three-quarters of a century. His son, Jim, the grandson of the founder, has worked there for nearly a half-century. Today, two of Jim's sons, great-grandsons of B. C. Clark, Coleman and Mitchell Clark, help lead the business as well.

Through four generations, they have learned to work together as a team; each member dedicated to the company's founding principles and each one serving with personal excellence. The family cares about each other and the reputation they have developed in the community. At the same time, each member of the team is making a unique contribution.

One early feature of the store's marketing campaign is a unique sales jingle, which now has its own fan page on social media sites and a downloadable ringtone. It is featured only from Thanksgiving to Christmas, and has been used every year since 1956 without exception, becoming one of the trademarks of the city.

> *Jewelry is the gift to give,*
> *'Cause it's the gift that'll live and live.*
> *So give the gift that cannot fail,*
> *From B. C. Clark's anniversary sale . . .*

Today the commercials feature local teams, school chorales, TV stars, and even the Sweet Adeline's singing the familiar song. It even receives fan mail from customers living overseas.

The younger generation of Clarks has added their own ideas. For instance, the last several years they have done a promotion for people buying engagement rings. If a couple purchases their wedding and engagement rings at B. C. Clark and it rains an inch or more on their wedding day, the cost of the rings is refunded up to five thousand dollars. The promotion has been highly successful, with local news stations doing stories featuring couples that have received free rings. And the free publicity generated is probably worth more than the cost of the rings.

B. C. Clark pledges to carry only the finest jewelry. It is continuously recognized in survey after survey as the best jewelry store in Oklahoma, receiving national recognition for their expertise in the field as well as for the quality of service to their customers.

Community That Works

These three companies, JetBlue, eBay, and B. C. Clark, are very different; yet all of them practice similar principles of teamwork.

> The leaders of the companies understand the definition of teamwork as it applies uniquely to their organizations.

For example, a basketball team will work together differently from a baseball team, which will work differently from a football team. But, in each sport, each member of the team understands his or her role as it relates to the team.

The same is true of the business organizations mentioned. At JetBlue, teamwork means doing whatever is necessary to fulfill its mission, whether flying airplanes, maintaining equipment, or handling the baggage. At eBay, many employees will never meet other members of the team, but they will use technology to communicate with the team, and stay focused on facilitating sales and service. At B. C. Clark, members of the family and their staff commit to seeing lives change as they sell jewelry to commemorate life's big events.

Toni Carter is on that same worker wavelength. Working at Taco Bell has made her a member, not only of a community of customers, but of the whole staff as well. She is part of a team of employees, each playing their part to make the fast food experience a good one for the customers.

True, Toni has limitations due to her medical conditions but she has many strengths. And her manager knows . . .

It is always better to put someone in a position where they can succeed with their strengths than to try to improve on their weak areas.

Toni's strengths are her smile and outgoing personality. Her roles—refilling soft drinks, handing out napkins and straws, wishing each customer a good day—are no less important than those who are preparing the food or handling the money.

Toni also has the talent to create community among those eating at her Taco Bell. Because of her personal attention, many have made her Taco Bell their fast food choice.

The Game plan:
Definition, Assessment, Accountability

Each team's definition of teamwork is unique to that organization, but important in its own way. No one can be a strong member of the team if they do not understand the team's objective and how it is going to reach its individual goals. Teamwork must be well defined in the mind of everyone in the organization. If someone on the team is asked what the team is trying to achieve and how they are going to do it, the answer from everyone—custodian to the CEO—should be much the same.

On a football team, part of the team can't be playing "run-and-gun" while another plays a wishbone offense. Both strategies might be successful, but they cannot operate simultaneously. Whatever the sport, a successful team will have a defined game plan, and every player will understand, and in business, its the same.

A successful organization also uses a predetermined method to assess the quality of its teamwork. The assessment tool will vary from team to team. For instance, JetBlue may assess whether or not their planes are leaving on time and getting their passengers where they need to be in a timely manner. That assessment may be expanded to include handling lost luggage or other individual needs of their passengers.

- eBay may assess the number of products they are selling and measure the ease with which products are transitioning from seller to buyer.

- B. C. Clark will look at their product line—everything from wedding rings to gifts to watches—and assess whether or not their customers' needs are being met with total quality.

- In sports, the assessment may be broadly done through the win-loss record. But on a deeper level, real assessment involves determining the role of every team member in the success, or failure, of the team.

Assessment is a vital part of the teamwork process, and it can help strengthen even the weakest team member.

Once the team leaders have completed the assessment phase, they must create an action plan to build up the weak areas. In sports, it may involve anything from weightlifting to learning plays to batting practice. In business, it may involve anything from additional training to a mentoring program to team-building exercises.

After the assessment, each member has to be held accountable for his or her job or the whole team suffers. In sports, being held accountable can be a very public matter. For example, in professional football when a player commits a foul his number is called and his mistake announced over the sound system.

Accountability in the business world may not be quite as public, but it is no less real. When deadlines are missed, work not completed, orders not filled, or products not available, the organization is impacted in negative way. Sometimes the effects seem small—a matter of customer complaints that are not highly publicized. Other times, when laws are broken or ethical standards violated, the effects may be very public with hearings or arrest warrants.

Sometimes management is slow to hold people accountable because of morale issues or employee reprisal. But, actually, everyone wins when each member works equally for the success of the team.

In the state where I (Keith) live, the Ohio State Buckeyes are renowned for their success on the gridiron. More than once a freshman has walked on the campus and has beaten out an upperclassman for a position. When questioned, the coach usually reminds everyone that the team is only as successful as the weakest player. As business leaders, we may not replace our team members as often as a sports team, but the assessment of team members is no less important.

Family teams usually work well together because they know nearly everything about each other. In a similar way, its customers and employees become like a team through years of doing business together. For example, good salespeople often anticipate the likes and dislikes of their customers, and sometimes hold products back when items arrive in the store because they know they would appeal to them. The salesperson provides personal service for the customer, and the customer provides loyalty to the salesperson. It is a win-win for everyone.

Customer Loyalty

Loyal customers are similar to football fans. Every Saturday during the fall season, these committed souls gather by the tens of thousands to watch their collegiate sports heroes. Hundreds of millions of dollars have been spent on sports arenas and stadiums. Boards or committees may debate for hours over whether to spend a few hundred dollars on a coat of paint for a college's administration office, but approve millions of dollars for a sports team on a voice vote.

Fifty years ago legendary coach Bud Wilkinson of Oklahoma University earned more money than its President. When the regents were questioned about their priorities, they responded, "Bud had a better year."

Enough said.

In retail, loyal customers do not desert stores for a little better price or a fancier model. In today's competitive environment, many business owners seem to downplay the importance of building a community of customers through quality service in lieu of building a quantity of customers through discounted prices.

One of the greatest examples of customer loyalty in the twenty-first century is Apple Inc.

The giant retailer spends a smaller portion of its revenues on advertising than its competition. It charges a higher price for its products, and makes a higher profit per unit. Many of its competitors are in survival mode, while Apple's revenues keep rising every quarter.

Apple customers actually stand in line to pay a premium price for products they may have never touched and may have barely seen. When interviewed, they claim to feel privileged for the wait.

However, it is more than the product itself that draws them. Apple customers feel a certain relationship with each other. This is customer community at its best: people sharing the things in life they value.

The intensity of that sense of community is amazing. According to Harvard Business Review, companies whose customers' affinity goes beyond loyalty to love can charge 15 percent more than their competitors for their premium services.

In difficult times, businesses and organizations may think about cutting back—eliminating personal services, and even some services or product lines altogether. But the greater chance for success lies in simply providing more and better service. Whether it is a store, a company, or a church, any entity can become community if it draws people together.

Corporations recognize that customer loyalty is gold. The customer who returns time and time again is the customer every merchant wants. But,

Loyalty is earned—not bought.

Positive customer experience results in return visits. Teamwork is an important part of that experience—providing excellent customer service and working in sync with each other.

The story is told of Bonnie, a former missionary and faculty member of a well-known Christian college, who lost a years-long battle with cancer.

The last days of her life were full of celebrating her wins. Instead of mourning her losses, she gathered her beloved family and a few college friends for a vacation at the ocean. It was a week of joyously celebrating the past victories and prayerfully anticipating the future. The laughter-filled days were juxtaposed with days of debilitating discomfort.

In the days following her funeral, the college president reflected on Bonnie's life of service. She said the former missionary and founder of a compassionate ministries organization made a difference in the world "as only she could make." Her unique gifts were listed as those things she had made "available to God for His purpose." They were impressive:

The ability to make people feel at home,

The gift of paying attention,

The gift of asking questions,

The gift of celebration . . .

They were pillars that formed a tower of strength—along with her other gifts, such as her organizational ability, persistence, and encouragement.

A team member was lost on that cold winter day. But the warm rays of her and care for others is a light that will continue to shine through those she had served and those she had trained to serve.

Uncommon customer service isn't limited by the special needs of those who, in spite of their own concerns, care for others. In fact, their challenges propel them to even higher achievement. Look at their lives, and then look around.

Customer service is the custom of serving others.

CHAPTER SIX
Communication: A Story to Tell

The man who will use his skill and constructive imagination to see how much he can give for a dollar, instead of how little he can give for a dollar, is bound to succeed. - Henry Ford

Author and seminar speaker, Terry Bates, loves to tell the story about the time he was waiting in a rental car line to get his car. Apparently, the line was long and no one was being served. A man in the front of the line observed several employees standing and talking behind the counter and said, "With all those people behind the counter, can't someone help us?"

Terry said the manager looked up and remarked, "Are you talking to me? 'Cause if you're talking to me, I ain't listening!" Now there's a breakdown in communication between the customer and the server!

The final "C"— but arguably the most important—is communication. Without communication there can be no effective customer service. As we know, communication is much more than simply speaking. In fact, speaking and listening combined is not the full extent of what it means to communicate. John Woods once said, "You can't *not* communicate. Everything you say or do—or don't say and don't do sends a message to others." The question is not whether we are going to communicate; but, will we communicate effectively?

After Kim Hawk suffered the stroke which would eventually claim her life, she was only able to say a few words— words she didn't have to think about, words that flowed naturally from her heart. They included "Mom," "I love you," and "Terrific!" She communicated words that had been a part of her for all of her life. Positive, encouraging words came naturally to Kim because they were a part of her daily communications. How much more should such words flow from you when you are with others?

Everyone involved with a customer has to understand that there are barriers that must be overcome to make the sale. *First, people don't trust you.* They don't know enough about you to form a positive opinion. *Second, they aren't sure what they need.* Their first impression of our product or service is seed to be sown, not fruit to be harvested. *Third, they may know what they need but they are not sure they need you to meet that need. Fourth, things go wrong.* The customer service agent must deal with client satisfaction.

There are several high profile steps to effective communication—and subsequently good customer service:

1. Attitude

The first step doesn't necessarily have anything to do with speaking or listening; it has everything to do with attitude. It is the first thing a customer picks up from you before either of you says a word.

How many times have you conducted business with someone and sensed something about them before anything was said? We can smile without using our mouths. We can disapprove by a raised eyebrow or a shake of the head. We can be enthusiastic and encouraging before the business negotiation begins. If we are enthusiastic about the opportunity, the customer will be enthusiastic as well. But the opposite is also true. If we are unhappy or disapproving, that attitude will spill over to the customer as well.

A friendly smile can lift up anyone's situation, regardless of how difficult the day is. A large part of Toni Carter's popularity with her customers at Taco Bell is her big smile. She communicates a welcome as soon as they walk through the door. When they have placed their order she often shows them an open booth. She'll gladly get them napkins, straws and packets of Taco Bell's famous hot sauces. What do her actions communicate? It says, "You are valuable to us, and we are glad you chose to dine with us today."

The saying is true, "We are always communicating." Toni does this with her smile, with her welcoming words, and with her willingness to serve others. Everything she does communicates her desire to make a customer the center of her world for those few moments.

> A positive attitude from service personnel is an instant connector to the customer—and creates in them a spirit of expectancy, which may well result in sales or recruitment.

The attitude we bring to any situation will become known even without facial gestures. An individual may try to hide it, but it will still shine through. Entrepreneur Mary Kay Ash was known for her saying, "Everyone has an invisible sign hanging from their neck. It says, 'Make Me Feel Important.'" There is a reason that telemarketers will often work with a mirror at their desk while they talk on the phone. They know the smile on their face will travel through the phone to the customer. They practice having a great attitude by smiling at themselves in the mirror. Attitude is everything.

Are We Enthusiastic?

A business consultant tells of working with one of his biggest clients. While talking with some of the marketing people, he discovered they had the habit of making disparaging remarks about customers. The marketers were very smart people who cared about their products and customers; they had just fallen into a habit of putting the customers down when they weren't around. This was a good company with many positive attributes, but he knew this attitude was going to pull them down if they didn't reverse it.

The consultant spoke to the boss about the situation. At first, the boss thought the consultant was exaggerating the situation. He was sure that only some of his people were complaining about specific situations and that the problem was not universal. He was confident that his salespeople were generally positive about their customers.

However, the consultant courageously told the boss that the old adage of one bad apple spoiling the entire barrel was true, and if the attitude persisted with a few, it would eventually spread like a cancer to everyone in the company. If everyone adopted the attitude of a few, the situation would get worse.

The boss concluded that he could not let this happen and immediately told the consultant to do whatever he needed to rectify the situation. The consultant suggested they adopt a principle that companies have been using forever:

"Fake it, 'til you make it."

He encouraged the marketing department to fake being enthusiastic, to be positive even when they didn't feel like it. He even encouraged them to start their mornings by saying together, "Are we enthusiastic? Yes, we're enthusiastic!" This would be the equivalent of a telemarketer looking in the mirror to adopt a good attitude and putting a smile on his face whether he really feels like it or not.

The exercise seemed foolish to some. They didn't think they had a problem anyway—in their minds, by complaining about their customers, they were just entertaining each other with amusing anecdotes. But, to show their willingness to cooperate, they agreed to try. In the beginning, they felt silly. But the effort did cause them to be more aware of the things they said about their customers.

They found themselves catching demeaning statements that came out of their mouths. Soon the awareness of what they said about their customers became second nature, and saying good things became natural to them.

It wasn't long before everyone noticed an overall change of attitude in the company. The positive became contagious instead of the negative. There were no more water-cooler jokes and stories about the customers; instead everyone began to tell stories of good interaction with their customers. When issues did arise, people were quick to come up with innovations that improved the situation.

Further, it seemed to the employees that the attitude of the customers improved as well. Sales begin to improve without more advertising or marketing efforts. In the process, the marketing department learned that the best way to improve their job was to strive to have the best attitude possible while working with customers. In effect,

A good attitude toward customers changes everything.

2. Listening

Once the attitude is improved, the next step in communication is effective listening. Business guru Peter Drucker wrote, "The most important thing in communication is hearing what isn't said." So, the first step in listening is being silent. Most of us talk so much that we don't take the time to listen. Being quiet is more than simply not talking; it is also not thinking about what you want to say next. It is being quiet and listening intently to what the other person is saying, weighing each word.

Silence gives the person to whom you are listening, the personal space to relax and talk.

Few people can speak freely if they feel the need to be on the defense against your words; their mind is too cluttered with defending their personal space. Often when we listen, our heads are filled with our own thoughts, leaving little space for the thoughts of others. We must be open to the listening opportunity.

The path to clearing space in our minds is to rid ourselves of the urge to make judgments, or predict what people are going to do or say based on the way we've labeled them. Many times we are so busy anticipating what people are going to do or say that we don't really notice what is happening in front of us. We assume that everyone has the same beliefs, thoughts, and attitudes, and that we can anticipate their every move. But people can be very surprising and do the unexpected.

Years ago television personality Art Linkletter had a popular show called *Kids Say the Darnedest Things*. That phrase is true not only of children, but also of people of all ages and backgrounds. But it will take **Xtreme** listening to sort out the unusual from the mundane.

Listening requires undivided attention and focus. That's a difficult challenge in today's world of constant communication. Cell phones ring, restaurants have televisions blaring in every corner, people laugh and talk all around us. But when we give others space to talk, we may hear them say something that is profound and life changing—and in the process, develop loyalty from the person doing the talking.

Many organizations place extreme value on listening. It is built into their business philosophy. A good example of this is found in the service model of the restaurant giant, McDonalds. Irish public relations consultant Piaras Kelly quoted founder Ray Kroc's customer service doctrine that was re-purposed by James Richard Cantalupo, chairman and CEO of McDonalds Corporation until his sudden death of a heart attack at age 60.

Kroc's philosophy may have been an adaption of Mahatma Gandhi's writings. He was the revered national leader of India who sought to bring economic vitality to his country:

> "A customer is the most important visitor on our premises. He is not dependent on us. We are dependent on him. He is not an interruption in our work. He is the purpose of it. He is not an outsider in our business. He is part of it. We are not doing him a favor by serving him. He is doing us a favor by giving us an opportunity to do so."

McDonald's 10 Commandments of Customer Service

The revived customer service mottos adopted by Cantalupo illustrate why McDonalds has been so successful.

1. **The first statement was,** *"The customer is the most important person in our business."* So many businesses want to make their product the focus of the business. While they may have a great product, if no one buys it, its quality is irrelevant. McDonalds may not serve the biggest and best hamburgers in the world, but their customer service is well documented.

2. **The second motto for service is,** *"The customer is not dependent on us—we are dependent upon the customer."* When we realize that we ought to be focused primarily on satisfying the customer—and that it's not their duty to satisfy us—it changes the entire relationship. Sometimes employees and their bosses behave as though it is their task to please each other, not customers. But in business, if there are no customers there is no business.

In a global economy, customers almost always have multiple options from which to choose. When McDonalds first started hardly anyone was in the fast food business, but today there are many. If customers are not satisfied by one fast food place, they have plenty of options.

3. **The third motto is especially relevant to the business world today:** *"The customer is not an interruption of our work, but the purpose of it."* How many of us have stood in line and watched the clerk converse with a friend while the customer line grew? In those situations, the customers

feel they are an interruption to the business, not the purpose of the business.

4. The fourth statement is directly related to the third: *"The customer does us an honor when calling on us. We are not doing the customer a favor by serving him or her."* When the relationship between the business and the customer comes into proper focus, customer service becomes much less complicated. And employees begin to understand the appropriate motivation from which to provide excellent customer service.

5. The customer should be considered an integral part of business. *The customer is not an outsider, but a guest.*

That's the reason prosperous businesses as Disney World use the word "guests" instead of "customers"—it affects the attitude of their employees toward the customers.

6. The next affirmation from the McDonalds original motto is: *"The customer is not a statistic, but flesh and blood; a human with feelings and emotions like our own."* Too many organizations treat their customers as numbers and not as people. Unfortunately, for some companies the customers' likes and wants has very little to do with the decisions made regarding their products or services.

Instead, the customers are seen as sources of cash flow or revenue. The goal of the company becomes to generate the greatest amount of revenue, not to meet the greatest needs of the customer.

7. The next motto is a reminder that, *"The customer is not someone to argue with or match wits with."* Some companies instruct their employees to leverage sales by leading the customer to make decisions they do not really want to make. Those companies take the attitude that it is their job to convince customers to do what is best for the company, not to provide what is best for customers.

This leads to very dissatisfied customers who will take their business elsewhere at the first possible opportunity. It also runs completely counter to effective cash flow management and profit generation.

That's the standard for McDonalds cross-generational customer loyalty. Customers who once brought their children to McDonalds are now returning with their grandchildren.

The best money is made through satisfied, return customers who serve as word-of-mouth advertisers for the product or service.

8. Statements eight and nine are related as well: *"The customer is one who brings his or her wants. Our job is to fill them,"* and . . ,

9. *"The customer is deserving of the most courteous and attentive treatment we can provide."* The techniques of operating a business can be so simple, but leaders often make it so complicated.

The way to profitability and success is to find a need and fill it.

This is true in any business or organization in the world. If you can gather a supply of what people are demanding and find a way to provide it to them, you will be on the success track. For example, familiar telecommunication giants are losing business because they continue to push land line service to customers who have moved to the convenience of digital technology, such as Internet-based communications. It is simply supply and demand.

10. The tenth and final McDonalds motto is something that should be posted wherever people serve the customer face-to-face: *"The customer has the right to expect an employee to present a neat, clean appearance . . ."*

A customer's first impression is important. Not only does the employee's appearance reflect company values, it connects positively or negatively with the very customers who keep the company going. That alone is reason enough for employees to present themselves well to their customers. This does not necessarily mean that every employee has to wear a matching uniform. It simply means that they should dress appropriately and attractively.

Kroc, the former milkshake machine salesman who co-founded McDonalds, understood that excellent customer service means meeting the unspoken needs of their customers. The best customer service anticipates the needs of customers; the best customer service acts rather than reacts.

Too often by the time a company or individual employee reacts to a customer's situation, it is too late—he or she has solved the problem through other means. If the problem can be resolved somewhere else, the possibility of losing that customer grows exponentially.

The primary job of a company in providing a product or service is to address the needs and solve the problems of its customers.

Organizations must communicate a willingness to be there for the customer when the need arises. Several years ago, General Motors tried to make many of their car models similar because offering highly similar products was more cost efficient in the manufacturing process. The problem with this strategy was that GM was thinking about its own needs and not about the customer's. One of their competitors made a commercial that pointed out how many of their models looked alike.

By the time GM reacted, they had not only lost customers, they had lost a double-digit market share. Fortunately, they woke up to the reality that companies like Honda, Toyota and Hyundai had the answers to success in the car industry and made the adjustments to return to prominence.

3. Customer Feedback

Another aspect of good customer service is following up with them. All too often, follow-up with customers has become, "How can I sell you more?" not, "How can I serve you better?" Through good feedback from customers, business and organization leaders will gain the knowledge needed to measure what matters most. Follow up (or follow through) information can be gained from the answers in simple questionnaires following a transaction or service.

The key to getting the most out of customer feedback is to use it to appropriately measure why the customers were pleased or displeased with your product or service, and how your product or service made a difference to them.

> The better you know your customers, the more you will be equipped to please them; and the happier they are, the longer they will be loyal customers.

An excellent example of the importance of surveys and customer interviews is illustrated by Procter & Gamble. They surveyed households in the country of Mexico. One series of responses indicated that because of the lack of shelf space in the customers' homes, the best soap product would be in a concentrate form. They also learned that, because of the short supply of water, a detergent with enzymes that created less foam would be easier to rinse.

The responses were relevant to the company, but there was one problem: those surveyed didn't buy the product. When they followed up the survey, they learned that the responders were proud of their clean clothes, and the way they saw it, soap with more foam made the clothes cleaner. So in reality, shelf space didn't factor into their decision as much as the importance of clean clothes.

So, Procter & Gamble again changed their formula. They made a product that was less concentrated and produced more suds, sold it in a bigger box, and sales skyrocketed. All this happened because they were willing to ask people why they no longer purchased soap from the company.

Another step in providing quality customer service is to deliver on advertised promises, and then exceeding the expectations. It's easy for companies to put a positive spin on what they can do for customers. But, our culture has become so accustomed to spin that it is now expected. Spin doctors are often hired by public officials and companies to minimize damage when things go wrong. However, the best path is to avoid the spin by doing things right and meeting the expectations of the customer.

A few decades ago, there was an example of this principle. A car company built a compact car. The car became very popular because of its excellent gas mileage, and as a result, thousands of them were sold. However, some of the cars were involved in rear-end collisions and exploded, badly injuring or killing some of the car's occupants.

It was determined the cars had exploded because of the placement of the gas tank. The company engineers studied the issue and found a way to fix the problem. When the CEO was informed of the problem, he asked two questions:

- What will it cost to recall the cars and make repairs on the gas tank?

- What will be the anticipated cost of lawsuits coming from the deaths of people involved in these accidents?

It was determined that the cost of making the repairs to the gas tank and saving lives was greater than potential cost of settling the lawsuits. They decided against the recall and braced themselves for the lawsuits. Unfortunately, the amount of money the company lost due to bad public relations and poor public perception was incalculable. They apparently became more concerned about profits than people. And they were eventually forced by the government to do a recall anyway.

About the same time, Chrysler Corporation had an issue which affected their customer relations. Some of the Chrysler executives were routinely driving company cars for a while and then replacing them with new ones. Apparently, these executives decided that since their cars had low mileage and had received high quality maintenance, they would roll back the miles on the odometer—and sell the cars as new, with a full factory warranty.

When word leaked, it created a firestorm. Lee Iacocca, who was CEO of Chrysler at the time, took immediate action by placing full-page ads in major newspapers around the country. The essence of the ad was: *This happened, and we are truly sorry. The guys who did it have been fired, and it won't happen again.* The response from the public was overwhelmingly positive. And Iacocca was publicly lauded.

The other company with the compact car fiasco was featured in the news for years, and it cost them a great deal in public confidence. Chrysler's problem lasted less than a week, and become a public relations success.

Each company communicated something to their customers, and the messages were very different. One company sent a silent message of indifference. The other company sent a public message of concern.

4. Staying in Touch

The last step in our discussion of quality customer service is to stay in touch with your customers. In today's market, with myriad means for connection, it's easy to stay in touch with people. But it means being open and available to what the customer wants to communicate about the product they have purchased.

Communication is the essential tool of quality customer service.

We can't always give a presentation that can sell a solution, but we can anticipate the questions people will have about us.

It allows the organization to anticipate the needs of customers before they occur. It enlightens and engages the customer to be specific about what is being done right and what is going wrong with the consumer and/or the product. And, it provides insight to help the business develop new products and services which can lead to greater profitability. Communication is the key to five star customer service.

Customer Service and the Five Stars

We have already addressed the concept of five-star customer service, but it bears repeating. Our world population is ever-increasing, yet in another sense, our world has actually become smaller—we are more connected than ever before. International communication and corporate diversification is at the next level. This interconnection through trade and cross cultural services has enhanced our society ties. Political revolutions have occurred, for example, because governments cannot control communication as much as they once did.

But in other ways, these communication tools have also created barriers to effective customer service. For example, if a person wanted to complain about or praise a product or service, they could drive to a local business and talk to a live person. Now we speak via the Internet or a cell phone to someone who may or may not have any firsthand experience with the product or service mentioned. In today's high tech business world, the personal touch is almost as extinct as a phone booth.

Companies often have a difficult time understanding that good customer *service* results in loyal customer *sales*. And loyal customers, it turns out, are very cost effective. Companies will spend thousands of dollars attracting new customers and yet be losing the ones who matter the most.

A study was done by IBM and its affiliates to find new customers for Papa Gino's, a pizza restaurant in Boston. The data was impressive; analytics proved the customers were out there all right! But the study opened a new dimension: "Analytics helped them discover that reward members visit their restaurants 35% more frequently and spend 50% more on online transactions. With new insights into the impact of their loyalty program, they can develop offers based on purchase patterns to increase the size of orders and purchase frequency."

The good news is that any company can turn itself around and create excellence in their organization. During his popular seminars, productivity consultant Denis Waitley frequently quotes Booker T. Washington:

"Excellence is to do a common thing in an uncommon way."

It's true; methods have changed, but the need for excellence has not. People and companies who are willing to raise their standards and provide excellent customer service will be rewarded. The late Earl Nightingale once said, "We can let circumstances rule us, or we can take charge and rule our lives from within."

- Kim Hawk never allowed her life to be determined by her circumstances. She decided to be the master of her fate. She loved people and decided that she could make a difference in their lives by always having a winning smile and an encouraging word to share. She was determined to be the best that she could be. Our world would be a much better place if others adopted her attitude that "life is terrific!"

- Heather Duvall lives by her Eight Principles of Success as she works with other special needs children and adults; a smile is at the heart of her daily plan.

- Toni Carter gets to know her Taco Bell customers by name, smiles real big, and meets their needs before they even ask.

Successful five star customer service (*Terrific!* customer service) is always delivered with a helping hand and a winning smile.

Motivational speaker Zig Ziglar defined success as "The maximum utilization of the ability that you have."

Joe Knapp described it as "Living up to your potential. That's all. Wake up with a smile and go after life and live it; enjoy it, taste it, smell it, feel it."

Can we learn from those who struggle with learning disabilities? Of course!

Can we learn how to meet the needs of customers from those with special needs? Absolutely!

Millions of readers and YouTube viewers know him as Johnny the Bagger. Authors Ken Blanchard and Barbara Glanz told his story in the book, "The Simple Truths of Service." Johnny was a nineteen-year-old grocery bagger whose heart for others gained world-wide attention.

Glanz, a motivational speaker, was asked to speak to the employees of a major grocery store chain. Following her presentation, an employee called the telephone number she had made available to the audience. He identified himself as a person with Down syndrome and said that he liked her talk. He added that he went home and asked his dad to help him with the computer in setting up a template in a document with three columns. Each day, he would add a thought for the day in the column rows—admitting that if he couldn't find one suitable, he made one up.

Each night he put the thoughts in the columns, made fifty copies, cut them out and put his name on the back of the slips of paper. Then, he began to put those daily thoughts in the store customers' bag of groceries.

Later the store manager called Barbara Glanz to tell her that the lines at Johnny's checkout lane were several times larger than any other lane. He said he called for more baggers but the customers said they WANTED to be in Johnny's line because they wanted Johnny's thought for the day.

Several months later the store manager called to tell Glanz that the simple act of service had transformed the store. Johnny's customer kindness was contagious. The young lady in the floral department began to collect the left over corsages and pin them on elderly ladies and young girls. The man at the meat counter ordered rolls of stickers with a picture of Snoopy on them and started adding them to the meat packages.

One young man, with challenges of his own, had a *Terrific!* customer service vision to communicate kindness to those he served. A store was transformed—but more importantly, lives were changed.

ABOUT THE AUTHORS

Stan Toler

Stan Toler has authored nearly one hundred books on leadership, spiritual growth, and personal improvement. His best-selling *Minute Motivators* series, filled with practical insights for family members and professionals, is available everywhere from online stores to big box discount stores, to retail stores to airport terminals around the world.

Used worldwide as a conference speaker, seminar leader, and corporate trainer, Stan's humble West Virginia roots influence the humorous and heartfelt stories in his messages and his best-selling books. His print and online writings have been translated into many languages and include such inspirational books as, *Give to Live, ReThink Your Life, Total Quality Life, Secret Blend*, numerous leadership kits and videos. Toler served as vice president and instructor for John C. Maxwell's INJOY leadership institute. For more information about Stan Toler, visit www.stantoler.com.

Left to Right: A.J. Hawk, Keith Hawk

Keith Hawk

Keith Hawk is the Senior Vice President of Sales – U.S. Legal & Professional markets, for LexisNexis, Inc. After 25 years in a wide variety of LexisNexis roles, (e.g., VP Sales, VP Customer Support, Director of Marketing, Director Technical Support, VP Client Relations), Keith has a very rich background in the electronic publishing industry, and he has played a broad role in the development of LexisNexis as a company. He is a public speaker who has worked with some of America's best companies and law firms in speaking and leadership consulting capacities.

Keith graduated from Ohio University in 1977 with a BS in Communications, and in 1987, received his MBA from the University of Dayton. He is married (Judy) and has 3 sons (Matthew, Ryan, A.J.). His hobbies include sports, writing, and speaking on business and leadership topics. His son, A.J. Hawk, plays professional football as a starting linebacker and captain for the NFL Super Bowl Champion Green Bay Packers. Keith's most recent book is titled, *Get-Real Selling: Your Personal Coach for REAL Sales Excellence*

A. J. Hawk

Born in Kettering, Ohio, on January 6, 1984, Aaron James Hawk grew up in Centerville with his parents, Keith and Judy, and older brothers, Matt and Ryan. He married Laura Quinn, sister of Denver Broncos quarterback Brady Quinn, in 2006, and they welcomed their daughter, Lennon Noel, in December 2010.

Hawk attended Centerville High School, leading the Elks to three consecutive league titles while earning All-State honors twice. A.J. still holds the school record for most tackles in a game (31)—a feat he accomplished three times—and in a career (583).

Hawk accepted a scholarship to the Ohio State University, starting 38 of the 51 games in which he appeared, recording 394 tackles in four seasons, including 196 solo stops, 41 tackles for a loss and 15 and a half sacks.

The Green Bay Packers selected A.J. with the fifth overall pick in the 2006 NFL Draft. In his first season, Hawk was selected as the NFL Rookie of the Week two times and led the Packers' defense with 120 total tackles, 83 of them solo. He finished third in voting for the Associated Press Defensive Rookie of the Year. In 2010 Hawk helped lead Green Bay to a Super Bowl title while earning his first Pro Bowl selection. - *www.ajhawk.com*

Notes

Notes

Notes

Notes

Notes